Straw into Gold

STRAW INTO GOLD
Books and Activities About Folktales

Jan Irving
and
Robin Currie

Illustrated by
Susie Kropa

Peddler's Pack Series No. 2

TEACHER IDEAS PRESS
A Division of
Libraries Unlimited, Inc.
Englewood, Colorado
1993

To BW and WM—
Living proof that
straw can still turn into gold.

TEACHER IDEAS PRESS
A Division of Libraries Unlimited, Inc.
P.O. Box 6633
Englewood, CO 80155-6633

Library of Congress Cataloging-in-Publication Data

Irving, Jan, 1942-
    Straw into gold : books and activities about folktales / Jan
Irving and Robin Currie ; illustrated by Susie Kropa.
        xii, 109 p. 22x28 cm. -- (Peddler's pack series ; no. 2)
    Includes bibliographical references and index.
    ISBN 1-56308-074-5 (softbound)
    1. Folklore--Study and teaching (Primary) 2. Activity programs in
education. 3. Libraries, Children's--Activity programs.
4. Folklore--Bibliography. I. Currie, Robin, 1948-   . II. Title.
III. Series.
GR45.I78   1993
398.21'071'2--dc20   93-30271
                                                              CIP

Contents

Introduction

Folktales are rich, creative sources for storytellers and teachers. They are the first stories we hear as children and they remain with us all of our lives. Because folktales have strong plots with definite structures and repeated refrains, they are natural for oral storytelling, and for children just beginning to read on their own. Teachers who wish to find stories that predict outcomes will find that folktales are appropriate. When children begin to write stories, they often have trouble knowing how to begin and end. The stock beginnings and endings in folktales will help. Because folktales often use a cumulative pattern or definite sequence, they are relatively easy for children to imitate in writing their own versions.

Since folktales from around the world provide insights into people and their diverse beliefs, studying them promotes cultural awareness. Most of the folktales we have included in this book have different versions in cultures around the world. Children will learn that there is not just one prototype for the stories, but many different ways to tell a similar story with the details changing as the specific culture dictates.

Straw into Gold features eight popular folktale patterns with our own new story versions and literature enrichment activities. The eight folktale patterns featured here are the Gingerbread Boy, The Three Pigs, The Three Bears, Cinderella, The Frog Prince, Red Riding Hood, Jack and the Beanstalk, and Soup Stories (Stone Soup and Wonderful Porridge).

The chapters are arranged in parallel fashion. After an introduction to each tale, there is an annotated booklist followed by our own retelling of the traditional tale, using media enhancement. We have included ways to use flannelboard, tube stories, draw-and-tell, object stories, puppet stories, and circle stories. Most of these methods are interactive so children will learn through participation.

After each traditional tale, we have included a new story version of our own. Our new version basically has the same story or plot, but it may have different characters, a different setting, and use some different motifs. A motif is a recurring element or theme in a folktale such as a magic pot, a wish, or a runaway food. Each new story version can be photocopied by the teacher for students to use in creating a script for readers theatre or a complete play.

The next section of each chapter, "Literature Enrichment Activities," begins with writing activities giving students opportunities to develop their own creative responses. There are chants, action rhymes, and songs to extend the stories. Our activities are interactive, inviting children to participate. For example, we may give a beginning stanza, leaving the activity open ended for students to complete on their own. Related crafts and games follow.

A suggestion for a skit is included in each chapter so that students will be encouraged to create their own stories. Margaret Read MacDonald's *The Skit Book* (Linnet, 1990) defines a skit as a short entertainment without lines, but with a plot outline from which the "actors" ad lib the lines. We have included stock lines and suggestions for costumes and props as appropriate.

The last section of each chapter refers to folktale versions and activities from our other books when appropriate.

Many outstanding picture book versions of folktales have been published in recent years so teachers and librarians will enjoy sharing the many versions of each story to compare and contrast. Children will learn to make distinctions between the versions and create stories of their own.

The straw of the folktale becomes gold with each new generation's retelling.

I.
Gingerbread Boy
Stories
and Activities

Run, Run, I'm on My Way

Food that runs away is funny even to very youngest children because they realize right away that fun is intended. When the gingerbread boy (or pancake) brags too much, the over-confident food is eaten. Because children overstep bounds themselves as they test limits, they understand the story's playful message.

There are many versions of the classic story of the gingerbread boy (or pancake) that runs away from its creator. In one of the best-known the gingerbread boy repeated the same refrain as he runs away from a series of people and animals: "Run, run, as fast as you can. You can't catch me. I'm the Gingerbread Man." In the end, he is tricked and eaten by a clever fox.

This story provides many opportunities for teachers and librarians. Children will enjoy creating new adventures for the gingerbread boy by writing other stories featuring different foods, possibly from many cultures. Variants and other versions of this tale listed in the bibliography include the Norwegian pancake boy, the Russian bun, and the Appalachian johnnycake story written in the folktale tradition. We have created a new version of these runaway food stories, "The Flying Space Bagel," and encourage students to write their own imaginative tales.

Booklist

Asbjørnsen, P. C., and Jørgen Moe. *The Runaway Pancake*. Translated by Joan Tate. Illustrated by Otto Svend. Larousse, 1980.

After a mother makes a pancake for her seven hungry children, the pancake rolls away past a series of farm animals. Piggy Wiggy tricks the pancake into sitting on his snout so he can eat it.

Brown, Marcia. *The Bun*. Harcourt Brace Jovanovich, 1972.

Based on the Russian tale, an old woman makes a bun that rolls away, meets a hare, a wolf, a bear, and a fox who tricks the bun in the end.

Cauley, Lorinda Bryan. *The Pancake Boy*. Putnam's, 1988.

Based on the Norwegian folktale, Goody Poody makes a pancake for her seven hungry children, but the pancake rolls away. The series of people and animals the pancake eludes includes Manny Panny, Henny Penny, Cocky Locky, Ducky Lucky, Goosey Poosey, and finally, Piggy Wiggy, who tricks the pancake. A recipe for sweet-milk pancakes is included.

Galdone, Paul. *The Gingerbread Boy*. Seabury, 1975.

A little old woman bakes a gingerbread boy for her husband, but as she takes him from the oven, the boy runs away. He also escapes from a cow, a horse, some men threshing wheat, and a field of mowers. Finally, a fox persuades the gingerbread boy to climb on his back to get across a stream. In the end, the gingerbread boy is eaten.

Jacobs, Joseph. *Johnny-Cake*. Illustrated by Emma L. Brock. Putnam's, 1933.

The johnnycake, a thick pancake baked in an oven, rolls past a boy, his parents, several workers, a bear, and a wolf. Finally, a fox tricks him by pretending not to hear well, so the johnnycake has to come closer to brag about how he has escaped from the others. When the johnnycake is close enough, the fox eats him.

Lobel, Anita. *The Pancake*. Greenwillow, 1978.

A woman with seven hungry children cooks a pancake, but just as she is ready to flip it, the cake jumps out of the pan and rolls away. A merry chase of people and barnyard animals pursues the pancake until it is eaten by a pig.

Pomerantz, Charlotte. *Whiff, Sniff, Nibble and Chew: The Gingerbread Boy Retold*. Illustrated by Monica Incisa. Greenwillow, 1984.

This verse variant of the gingerbread boy tells the story of an old woman baking the gingerbread boy for her brother. The treat runs away from them, a moo cow, an oink pig oink, and a fat cat fat. When he returns home, the old man gobbles it down in one bite, but the gingerbread boy jumps back out of the old man and runs away with the old woman.

Sawyer, Ruth. *Journey Cake, Ho!* Illustrated by Robert McCloskey. Viking, 1953.

When the farm falls on hard times, Johnny is sent on his way with a johnnycake. On the journey, the johnnycake bounces out and gives Johnny and the barnyard animals a merry chase. The rollicking rhyme and rhythmic prose adds to the fun of this story told in folktale style.

Scieszka, Jon. "The Stinky Cheese Man," *The Stinky Cheese Man and Other Fairly Stupid Tales*. Illustrated by Lane Smith. Viking, 1992.

This collection of stories, rewritten with outlandish details and endings, includes the story based on the Gingerbread Boy format called "The Stinky Cheese Man." A stinky cheese man runs away from a little old lady, a little old man, a cow, a little girl, and a little boy who don't mind his hasty retreat. A fox gives the smelly morsel a ride across the river, gags and sneezes, in the process throwing the stinky cheese man into the river.

Traditional Story with Media Enhancement

Using the patterns on pages 5 and 6, cut out the puppets from lightweight posterboard or old file folders and attach a craft stick to each puppet with tape. You may have children hold up the puppets as you retell the traditional story (a shortened version is told here), or you may place the puppets on the glass top of an overhead projector. When you turn on the light of the projector, the shapes will be projected on the wall as shadows. Move the puppets across the glass as the story suggests.

This version changes the refrain of the gingerbread boy to the option of singing the repeated lines to the tune of "Farmer in the Dell." Or you may use the traditional refrain as follows:

> Run, run as fast as you can.
> You can't catch me. I'm the gingerbread man!

The Gingerbread Boy

Once upon a time there was a little old woman and a little old man who loved gingerbread. One day the little old woman decided to make a special gingerbread boy for the little old man. She rolled out the dough and cut out the gingerbread boy. She put raisins down the front for buttons. She put raisins on the face for eyes and for a mouth, and a red candy for a bright red nose. Then she baked the gingerbread boy in the oven. It smelled so good, she could not wait to take a peek.

But when the little old woman opened the oven door, the gingerbread boy jumped out and ran around the room. The little old woman chased him, and the gingerbread boy sang out:

> Gingerbread Boy Song
> (Tune: "Farmer in the Dell")
>
> Out the door and over the hill
> I'm running fast and speedy
> I'm the jolly gingerbread boy
> Run! You can't catch me!

Well, the little old woman and the little old man ran after the gingerbread boy, but he ran out of the house, down the walk, and into the field.

A big brown cow saw the gingerbread boy and started to chase him. But the gingerbread boy sang out:

> Out the door and over the hill
> I'm running fast and speedy
> I'm the jolly gingerbread boy
> Run! You can't catch me!

The gingerbread boy ran and ran, and he ran away from the cow. He ran into the pasture.

A frisky horse saw the gingerbread boy and started to chase him. But the gingerbread boy sang out:

> Out the door and over the hill
> I'm running fast and speedy
> I'm the jolly gingerbread boy
> Run! You can't catch me!

The gingerbread boy ran and ran and ran away from the horse. He ran to another field. There in the field were men threshing the wheat. The threshers chased the gingerbread boy. But the gingerbread boy sang out:

> Out the door and over the hill
> I'm running fast and speedy
> I'm the jolly gingerbread boy
> Run! You can't catch me!

The gingerbread boy ran and ran, and ran away from the threshers. He ran to a stream. There in the stream was a fox. Now, the gingerbread boy didn't want to jump in the stream, but he saw the threshers and the frisky horse and the big brown cow behind him.

So when the fox offered to take the gingerbread boy across the stream on his back, the gingerbread boy agreed. First he jumped on the fox's back. Then, when the water got deeper, he jumped on the fox's head. And when the water was almost up to the fox's head, the gingerbread boy jumped right into the fox's mouth. And that was the end of the gingerbread boy.

MOUNT FIGURES ON CRAFT STICKS.
USE WITH OVERHEAD PROJECTOR
FOR SHADOW PLAY.

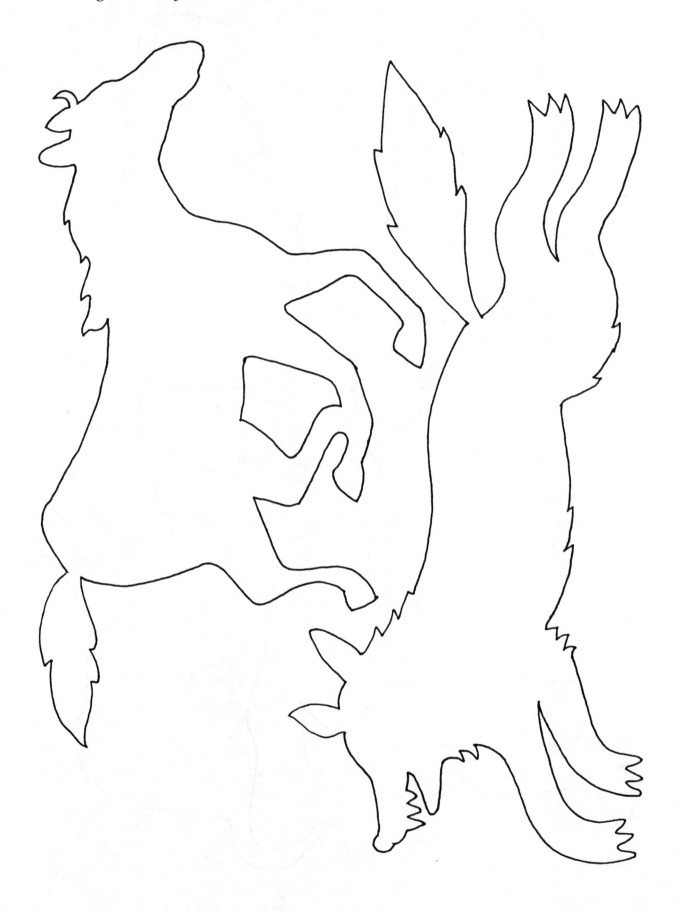

The Flying Space Bagel
(new story version)

Barney the Bagel Baker loved to make bagels in his shop, Barney's Bagel Bakery. All day long he made bagels—plain bagels, onion bagels, cinnamon bagels, and extra big bagels for bagel lovers.

One day Barney made the very biggest bagel he had ever made. He put it in the oven and it smelled so good that he opened the oven door to take a peek. But when the door was opened the very biggest bagel rolled out of the oven and onto the floor.

Barney the Baker shouted, "Come back here, you extra big bagel. I'm a bagel lover and I want to eat you!"

But the very biggest bagel said, "I won't let you take a bite. I'm off and rolling out of sight!"

The very biggest bagel rolled out the door, down the street, and into a gutter.

In the gutter it met a slimy sewer rat. The sewer rat sniffed the very biggest bagel and snarled, "Come back here, you big bagel. I'm a bagel lover and I want to eat you!"

But the very biggest bagel said, "I won't let you take a bite. I'm off and rolling out of sight!"

The very biggest bagel rolled down an alley. At the end of the alley were garbage cans and a fat alley cat. The fat alley cat sniffed the very biggest bagel and yowled, "Come back here, you big bagel. I'm a bagel lover and I want to eat you!"

But the very biggest bagel said, "I won't let you take a bite. I'm off and rolling out of sight!"

The very biggest bagel rolled into the city park. There it met a flock of pigeons. The pigeons swooped down on the bagel and squawked, "Come back here, you big bagel. We are bagel lovers and we want to eat you!"

But the very biggest bagel said, "I won't let you take a bite. I'm off and rolling out of sight!"

But no matter how fast the bagel rolled, the pigeons could fly faster. Finally, the bagel rolled so fast it rolled up off the ground and up, up, into the sky!

The pigeons flew after it. The bagel went spinning across the sky. The pigeons flew after it. The bagel spun faster and faster, higher and higher, until the pigeons could not chase it anymore.

The bagel went up spinning. Up past the tallest building. Up past the city smog. Up and into space. Why, that bagel became the very first flying space bagel!

The bagel called back to the baker, the sewer rat, the alley cat, and the flock of pigeons, "I won't let you take a bite. I'm off and rolling out of sight!"

Now, up in the sky was the very biggest bagel lover of them all. He was even round like the bagel. He was the man in the moon. When the bagel rolled by, the man in the moon smiled to himself.

The bagel started to brag again, "I won't let you take a bite, ..." Those were the last words he ever said. The man in the moon swallowed the very biggest bagel. Then he smiled again and said, "Wasn't that a pretty sight? I ate that bagel in just one bite."

Literature Enrichment Activities

Writing Activity

Class Cookbooks

Kids like to write their own versions of recipes. Let them create their own versions of gingerbread boy cookies that will be so good that everyone will want to eat them as fast as they can. The object of this activity is not to write authentic recipes, but for younger children to express themselves imaginatively. However unusual the outcome is, children are learning the process of listing quantities, measurement, and sequencing.

Compile all the recipes into a class cookbook.

Here's a sample recipe.

Good Gingerbread Boy

1 c sugar
2 c gingerbread dough
3 gobs of redhots
4 heaps of sprinkles
5 glasses of milk (save some to drink)

Mix together and cut into a gingerbread boy shape. Bake about 500 degrees for about one hour. Lock the oven so he can't run away!

Writing and Speaking Activity

Fun with Roll-Away Food

Use the following questions to do a group writing of a variant of the gingerbread boy. Determine the setting and characters. Write all responses on a chalkboard then have students complete the story in small groups. After all groups have written their versions, students read or act out the story for everyone.

Our example takes place in the American Southwest where many people enjoy tortillas. You might consider Chinese egg rolls, English scones, or Italian meatballs.

Planning the Roll-Away Tortilla Story

1. Who makes the tortilla? (Give him or her a name and brief description.)

2. What does this person always say? (Remember, this line will be repeated by all the other animals and people who chase the tortilla.)

3. What does the tortilla always reply? (This is usually a two line rhyme such as "Ole! I'm on my way!")

4. What three animals does the tortilla roll away from? (Brainstorm kinds of animals that are likely to live in the Southwest.)

5. Who catches the tortilla? (Think of a "trick" the animal would use. The best response we ever got to this question came from a sixth-grader who said a tortoise should be the one to catch the tortilla. In order to trick the tortilla, the tortoise crawled inside its shell. Then, when the tortilla rolled by, the tortoise stuck its head out and ate it!)

Speaking Activities

Gingerbread Boy
(chant)

The teacher or leader says the line first (breaking at the asterisk), then motions for the children to repeat the line. Children also repeat the leader's actions.

Gingerbread Boy
Out of the pan (clap hands)*
Took off
Ran! (slide one hand over the other as if running)*

Ran past a woman (slide one hand over the other as above)*
Ran past a man (slide one hand over the other as above)*
Come and catch me
If you can! (Wiggle fingers, moving head and hands from side to side as if taunting)*

Ran past a cow (slide one hand over the other as above)*
Ran past a cat (slide one hand over the other as above)*
Ran past some chickens (slide one hand over the other as above)*
And a big brown rat (clap three times)*

Came to a river*
Couldn't swim (shake head)*

Fox said,
"I will help you in." (Pat back three times)*

Gingerbread boy
Jump! (Clap)
Sly old fox (Shake pointing finger three times)*
Ate him up! (Clap once)

Pancake Song
(Tune: "This Old Man")

Use this song with the book *The Pancake* and sing it as a round. It is short enough for young children to learn quickly. For a reading activity, write the words on a transparency so children will be encouraged to read it as well.

> Pancake flat, pancake round
> Pancake rolling on the ground
> Rolling uphill, downhill
> Rolling merrily
> Calling out,
> "You can't catch me!"

Pizza to Go
(Tune: "Twinkle Twinkle Little Star")

Use this song along with a new version of the Gingerbread Man that you create with your students. Use the pattern "The Roll-Away Tortilla" on pages 8-9, but suggest a pizza instead of the tortilla.

> I'm a pizza made of dough
> Ready and all set "to go."
> Made of pepperoni, cheese,
> Olives, peppers, anchovies.
> I won't let you take a slice
> Even if you're very nice!

Related Crafts

Stuffed Gingerbread Kid

Children can trace the gingerbread kid pattern on page 11 onto a brown paper bag and cut out two shapes. They may decorate with buttons and yarn trim. Punch holes 1 inch from the outside edges. (See illustration.) Place the shapes on top of each other and use thick yarn to "sew" the shapes together. When the sewing is half finished, stuff the sewn part with scraps of newspaper, cotton balls, or facial tissue. Finish sewing and stuffing to make a plump gingerbread kid.

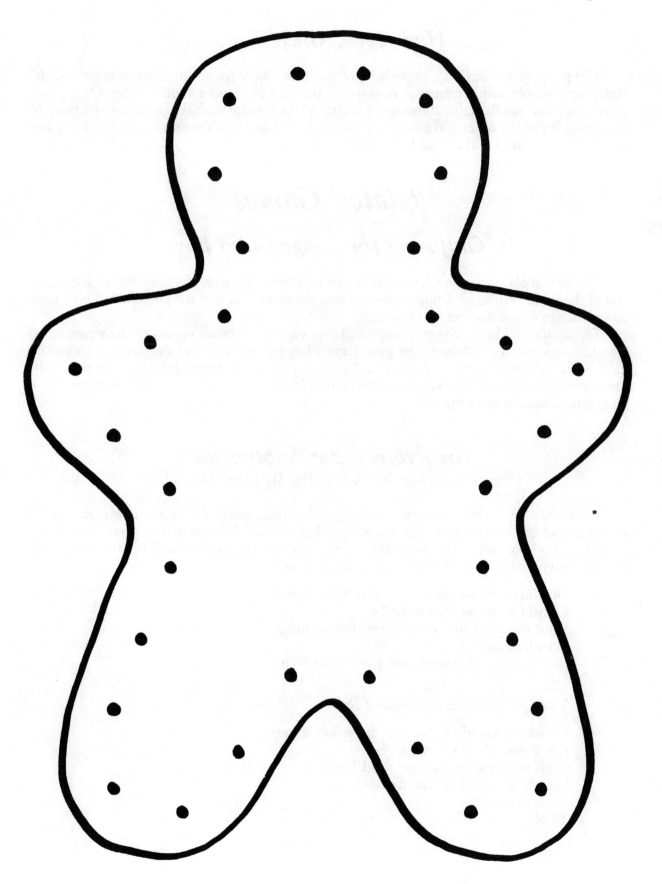

High Tech, Great Taste

Gingerbread persons may be a thing of the past—now we are into gingerbread robots! Make these simple edible treats out of three graham crackers and a vanilla wafer. On a paper plate, place the vanilla wafer above one graham cracker square to make the head and body of the robot. Break the other two cracker squares in halves to make arms and legs. Use icing and cookie decorations to add all the high-tech gear necessary for the gingerbread of tomorrow.

Related Games

Outfoxing the Gingerbread Boy

Before you play this game, have children recall what happens to the gingerbread boy at the end of the traditional story. Children should be able to tell you that the gingerbread boys ends up on the fox's nose just before he is eaten.

Divide the children into two groups and give each a cardboard cutout of the gingerbread boy. Children race by balancing the gingerbread boy on the nose and running to designated spot. After shouting "gulp," they race back and pass the gingerbread boy to the next person. The winning team is the first one to give everyone a chance to outfox the gingerbread boy. Serve gingerbread cookies to everyone!

Gingerbread Boy Subtraction
(Tune: "Oh Where, Oh Where Has My Little Dog Gone?")

There are several ways to have fun with this subtraction game. For example, give each child a gingerbread boy cookie. Start with the song below and let children make up verses until the gingerbread boys are all eaten. As an alternative, you may use flannelboard figures and simply remove designated parts as the children create stanzas.

> Oh where, oh where has my ginger boy gone?
> Oh where, oh where can he be?
> With two arms so short and two legs so long,
> Oh where, oh where can he be?
> (Eat one arm or remove arm piece from board.)

You may want this culminating stanza at the end.

> Oh where, oh where has my ginger boy gone?
> Oh where, oh where can he be?
> With no arms, no legs, no head I see.
> Oh where, oh where can he be?
> (Rub stomach)
> YUM!

Related Skit

The Gingerbread Girl or Boy

Characters:

> woman
> man
> gingerbread girl or boy
> cow
> pig
> fox
> other gingerbread children

Plot: A woman buys a box of gingerbread cookies. When she opens it one jumps out. She and the man run after the gingerbread boy. The cow chases the gingerbread boy. The gingerbread boy pulls the cow's tail and runs away from him. When the pig chases the gingerbread boy, he pinches the pig's snout and runs away from him. Then the gingerbread boy scares the fox by hiding in the bushes and yelling "boo" at him. The fox runs into the forest and the gingerbread boy goes back to the house. He lets the other cookies out of the box so they can all run away.

Note: In this skit, the children know the basic story line and they create their own lines and dialogue as they think the characters might say to them. This open ended approach will give children an opportunity to develop thinking skills and learn more about improvisation. Simple props and costumes will add interest to this presentation. The gingerbread kids can wear cut out cookie figures hung around their necks. The arms and legs can be jointed with brad fasteners so they can move as the child runs. The cow, pig, and fox can have masks made out of paper bags or paper plates.

Related Gingerbread Boy Activities
(from other Irving and Currie books)

1. "The Gingerbread Girl," in *Raising the Roof* (Teacher Ideas Press, 1991), 193-195.

2. "The Gingerbread Kid," in *Full Speed Ahead* (Teacher Ideas Press, 1989), 9-12.

3. "Gingerbread Man Story with Masks," in *Mudluscious* (Libraries Unlimited, 1986), 134-137.

4. "Gingerbread Boy in Verse," in *Mudluscious* (Libraries Unlimited, 1986), 137.

5. "The Pancake Chase," in *Mudluscious* (Libraries Unlimited, 1986), 137.

6. "Lighter-than-Air Cake," in *Mudluscious* (Libraries Unlimited, 1986), 103-105.

II.
Three Little Pigs
Stories
and Activities

Blow Your House Down

In one of the most popular English "beast" tales, three pigs set out to make their way in the world, but their first efforts in settling down are unsuccessful. The story most familiar to young children features a wolf who blows down the straw house built by the first pig, and then blows down the stick house built by the second pig. The hairy villain next tries to trick the third pig by making arrangements to meet him outside the security of the brick house, but the clever piglet outsmarts the wolf in the end.

One of the "lessons" of this tale is that fast and sloppy work can have disastrous consequences. The story is simple in its structure and is often one of the first young children are told. The repeated lines are easy to learn and are an early introduction to rhyme and rhythm.

> "Little pig, little pig, let me come in."
> "Not by the hairs of my chinny chin chin."
> "Then I'll huff and I'll puff and I'll blow your house in."

Illustrators including Leslie Brooks, Margot Zemach, and James Marshall have enjoyed humanizing the animals. Some recent retellings feature lift-the-flap formats, and the story told from the wolf's point of view. Several important versions of the three pigs were published in 1989: *The Three Little Pigs* by James Marshall, *The Three Little Pigs and the Fox* by William H. Hooks, and the best-seller, *The True Story of the 3 Little Pigs!* by Jon Scieszka.

The story has appeared in our books *Mudluscious* (Libraries Unlimited, 1986) as a food story (the wolf sees the pigs as a source of pork chops), and in *Raising the Roof* (Teacher Ideas Press, 1991) as a house-building tale. The possibilities for new versions may be endless. "Three Pigs on a Whirlwind Tour" takes the pigs all around the world with the wolf as their tour guide. Children will be encouraged to continue the adventure by telling stories of their own.

Booklist

Celsi, Teresa. *The Fourth Little Pig*. Illustrated by Doug Cushman. Steck-Vaughn Publishers, 1992.

The story begins where the traditional Three Pigs ends: all three pigs are in the brick house. But now they are so afraid of the wolf they don't go out at all. When their sister, Pig 4, arrives, she has to convince them there are no wolves around and there is lots to see and do outside.

Cole, Joanna, compiler. "The Three Hares," in *Best Loved Folktales of the World*. Doubleday, 1982.

In this Turkish variant of the pig's tale, three hares are sent out into the world to fend for themselves. The first two dig holes for houses that allow the fox to break in. The third hare digs a deeper hole that will keep him safe.

Hooks, William H. *The Three Little Pigs and the Fox*. Illustrated by S. D. Schindler. Macmillan, 1989.

In this Appalachian tale, three pigs, Rooter, Oinky, and Hamlet, set off, one by one, to build houses. Mama advises them to watch out for that "mean, tricky, old drooly-mouth fox," build a safe house, and visit Mama. The fox outsmarts the first two pigs and locks them in his den. But the third pig, their sister Hamlet, traps the fox and sets her brothers free so they can all visit home and enjoy Mama Pig's fine cooking.

Jacobs, Joseph. *The Story of the Three Little Pigs*. Illustrated by Lorinda Bryan Cauley. Putnam's, 1980.

In this classic tale the three pigs build houses of straw, furze (a spiney shrub), and bricks. The wolf demolishes the first two houses. The owner of the brick house not only keeps his house intact, but he also devours the wolf in the end.

Lowell, Susan. *The Three Little Javelinas*. Illustrated by Jim Harris. Northland Publishing, 1992.

Set in the southwest and full of authentic language and details, these javelinas (wild hairy pigs) build homes of tumbleweed and sugorous (cactus sticks) which a coyote blows down. Finally they are safe in the adobe house belonging to the third little javelina, their SISTER.

Marshall, James. *The Three Little Pigs*. Dial, 1989.

Marshall adds whimsical touches to the traditional tale. The old sow reminds the pigs to write as they leave home. When the first pig says he'll buy straw to build his house, the straw man warns him, "That's not a good idea." The pig quickly replies, "Mind your own business, thank you." As the third pig sets a cooking pot in the fireplace, the reader notices a cookbook on "How to Cook a Wolf" casually placed on a side chair. This version will interest older children who think they are too old for this tale.

Scieszka, Jon. *The True Story of the 3 Little Pigs*. Illustrated by Lane Smith. Viking Kestrel, 1989.

This retelling of the traditional story, told from the wolf's point of view, explains that the real story is about a sneeze and a cup of sugar. As the wolf is making a cake for his granny, he runs out of sugar and goes to the houses of the pigs to borrow some. Because he has a cold, the wolf sneezes and the sneezes blow down the pigs' houses. Caught by the police, the wolf declares he was framed by reporters trying to sensationalize the story.

The Three Little Pigs. Illustrated by John Wallner. Intervisual Communications, 1987.

This simplified version of the traditional tale features large print, manipulatives, and lift-the-flaps to encourage beginning readers to read the story for themselves.

Zemach, Margot. *The Three Little Pigs*. Farrar, Straus & Giroux, 1988.

In this traditional retelling of the story, the wolf overcomes the first two pigs, but the third tricks him and enjoys wolf soup for supper.

Traditional Story with Media Enhancement

The storytelling prop for this retelling of the three pigs shown on page 19 is made from two posterboard circles. On one circle cut a wedge. Opposite the wedge attach a piece of Velcro. Make a wolf out of posterboard and attach Velcro to the back of this figure so it can be put on the circle. On the other circle show a pig with a straw house, a pig with a stick house, and a pig with a brick house. Make sure these pictures can be seen through the wedge when the circle with the wolf is placed on top of the circle with the pigs. Attach the circles at the center with a brad fastener. As you tell the story, show the pigs' houses. Then add the wolf and turn the top circle to reveal which pig the wolf is after.

Round and Round with the Three Pigs

At a time when pigs could walk and talk and build houses, there lived three little pigs. One day the mother pig sent them off into the world to live on their own. That meant the pigs had to build houses to live in.

(Turn circle to reveal straw house.) The first little pig met a man carrying straw. He bought it and built his house of straw.

(Turn circle to reveal stick house.) The second little pig met a man with a load of sticks. He bought them and built his house of sticks.

(Turn circle to reveal brick house.) The third little pig met a man with a heavy load of bricks. He bought them and built his house of bricks. It took a long time, but it was very sturdy.

Now also living nearby was the big bad wolf. (Attach wolf to circle with Velcro.) He heard about those three pigs and their new homes and decided to make some mischief. He went to the house of the first little pig. It was made of straw. (Turn circle to reveal straw house.)

He called, "Little pig, little pig, let me come in!"

The little pig answered, "Not by the hair of my chinny chin chin!"

The wolf yelled, "Then I'll huff and I'll puff and I'll blow your house in!"

So he blew and blew and blew and the straw house fell down.

The wolf went to the house of the second little pig. It was made of sticks. (Turn circle to reveal stick house.)

He called, "Little pig, little pig, let me come in!"

The little pig answered, "Not by the hair of my chinny chin chin!"

The wolf yelled, "Then I'll huff and I'll puff and I'll blow your house in!"

So he blew and blew and blew and the stick house fell down.

Now the wolf went to the house of the third little pig. It was made of bricks. (Turn circle to reveal brick house.)

He called, "Little pig, little pig, let me come in!"

The little pig answered, "Not by the hair of my chinny chin chin!"

The wolf yelled, "Then huff and I'll puff and I'll blow your house in!"

So he blew and blew and blew but the brick house did not fall down. He blew and blew and blew some more, but the brick house did not fall down. He gave one last big-as-he-could blow, and when the house still did not fall down, he crawled into the woods and was never seen again. (Remove wolf figure from circle.)

And the pig in the brick house lived happily ever after.

BOTTOM CIRCLE

TOP CIRCLE
HAS WEDGE CUT
OUT...attach
WOLF

Three Pigs Take a Whirlwind Tour

(new story version)

It was an exciting day for the three pigs when they received this notice:

YOU HAVE ALREADY WON!

The pigs had won the Porkbarrel Sweepstakes. The prize was three tickets on a Worldwide Whirlwind Tour. So they packed their bags and set off on Wolverine Airlines. They met their tour guide at the airport. His face was a little hairy. In fact, he looked a little familiar to the pigs, but as he was wearing dark glasses they couldn't really be sure.

The first stop was the Swiss Alps. One pig learned to yodel. One pig bought a cuckoo clock. And one pig went to a Swiss cheese factory. Then they all went skiing. Their tour guide showed them the highest peak. (Of course he didn't go skiing with them.) On the way down a terrible avalanche started right on the pigs' ski run. They did manage to get out safely by the hairs of their chinny chin chins. At the bottom of the slope they met some other skiers.

"What an avalanche!" said the pigs.

The other skiers said, "That is really strange. There hasn't been an avalanche here for 100 years."

When the pigs met up with their tour guide they noticed he was slightly out of breath, his face was a little hairy, and he had very sharp teeth. In fact, he looked a little familiar to the pigs, but as he was wearing dark glasses they couldn't really be sure.

The next stop on their tour was Hawaii. One pig went surfing. One pig learned to hula. One pig visited a pineapple plantation. And they all went to visit a volcano. Their tour guide showed them to the very top. (Of course he didn't stay to sightsee.) On their way back down they heard a great rumble and saw hot lava pouring out of the volcano. They did manage to get out safely by the hairs of their chinny chin chins. At the bottom of the volcano they met some local people.

"What an eruption!" said the pigs.

The local people said, "That is really strange. That volcano hasn't been active for 200 years."

When the pigs met up with their tour guide they noticed he was slightly out of breath, his face was a little hairy, and he had very sharp teeth. He also had a gruff voice. In fact, he looked a little familiar to the pigs, but as he was wearing dark glasses they couldn't really be sure.

The next stop was Egypt. One pig toured the pyramids. One pig took a trip on the Nile. One pig went to the tombs. And they all went to see the Sahara Desert. Their tour guide showed them a desolate spot. (Of course he didn't stay to watch.) While they were there, a terrible wind came up that started a sandstorm. They did manage to get out safely by the hairs of their chinny chin chins. At the edge of the desert they met a camel keeper.

"What a sandstorm!" said the pigs.

The camel keeper said, "That is really strange. We haven't had a sandstorm in this season for 300 years."

When the pigs met up with their tour guide they noticed he was slightly out of breath, his face was a little hairy, and he had very sharp teeth. He also had a gruff voice and big ears. In fact, he looked a little familiar to the pigs, but as he was wearing dark glasses they couldn't really be sure. But they were getting very suspicious.

They were even more suspicious when the last stop on the tour was Chicago. They read billboards on the way to their hotel. The first pig said, "Look at that sign: Chicago is the Windy City."

The second pig said, "Look at that sign, 'Chicago is the Hog Butcher of the World'."

The third pig said, "I've seen all the signs that I need. Our tour guide is the wolf!"

So when the tour guide came to take them to the Sears Tower, the pigs were ready. The first pig said, "This is our last night on the tour."

The second pig said, "Let's have a party!"

The third pig said, "But who will blow up all the balloons?" The tour guide took a balloon and began to blow and blow and blow.

"Great," said the first pig.

"You can really blow up balloons," said the second pig.

"We have a whole roomful for you to blow," said the third pig.

While the wolf was blowing up the balloons, the pigs got out by the hairs on their chinny chin chins. They took a quick tour of the Sears Tower and took the next flight home to their little brick house.

Now that they were safely home, the pigs enjoyed special treats from all their adventures. The room was filled with balloons from their trip to Chicago. They served Swiss chocolate, Hawaiian pineapple and Egyptian dates. And they wolfed down every bite.

Literature Enrichment Activities

Writing Activity

A Parade of Pig Homes

Bring in real estate ads so children will become acquainted with the format of this kind of advertising. Work with children in small groups as they write ads for the three pigs' houses for a parade of homes in your community. Drawings will accompany the ads.

Wording for a sample ad might look like this:

Straw House

This slightly used house is being sold as is. Owner must relocate. Unusual straw construction. Priced to sell.

Stick House

Don't pass up this early American model. Affordable with low down payment. Rock bottom price!

Brick House

Sturdy construction guaranteed to stand up under heavy winds and stress. Mint condition. Working fireplace. Quiet, comfortable neighborhood.

Speaking Activities

Three Pigs
(action rhyme)

Three little pigs	(Raise three fingers)
built houses in town	
Big Bad Wolf	
Tried to blow them down	(Blow)
First house of straw	(Raise one finger)
Second of sticks	(Raise a second finger)
But look at that third house	(Hand to forehead as if looking)
That's made of bricks!	(Raise two fists)
"Little pig little pig	
Let me come in"	(Hands around mouth as if calling)
"Not by the hair of my	
Chinny Chin Chin"	(Shake head)

The wolf huffed and he puffed	(Blow hard)
And he blew and he wheezed	
The piggy's straw house	
Fell flat as you please	(Clap hands)
"Little pig little pig	(Hands around mouth as if calling)
Let me come in"	
"Not by the hair of my	
Chinny Chin Chin"	(Shake head)
So the wolf huffed and he puffed	
And he blew and he wheezed	(Blow hard)
'Til the piggy's stick house	
Fell flat as you please	(Clap hands)
"Little pig little pig	(Hands around mouth as if calling)
Let me come in"	
"Not by the hair of my	
Chinny Chin Chin"	(Shake head)
So the wolf huffed and he puffed	
And he blew and he wheezed	(Blow hard)
But the third pig's brick house	
Stood strong as you please.	(Raise two fists)

Pig Squeal
(Tune: "Old MacDonald Had a Farm")

Young children can practice the song in groups, but older children will be able to sing the song in rounds. Divide the children into three groups to sing the parts of the three scared little pigs. The double e (ee) is meant to be elongated into a pig squeal.

Big bad wolf is scaring me—
Wants me for his meal.
Big bad wolf has long sharp teeth
Listen to me squeal!
With an ee-ee here and an ee-ee there,
Here an ee.
There an ee.
Everywhere an ee-ee.
Big Bad Wolf is scaring me—
EE-EE-EE-EE-EE!

Wolf's Lament
(Tune: "Oh Where, Oh Where Has My Little Dog Gone?")

Oh where, oh where has that little pig gone?
Oh where did he run away?
I blew his house down,
But he just can't be found.
I wish he would come back to stay.

Related Craft

Build-Your-Own Pig House

Using the pattern below, design your own pig house with found objects, catalog pictures, or fabrics and trims. This collage project will make a good room decoration.

Related Games

Blow the House Down
(Tune: "London Bridge")

Sing this song as you play the traditional London Bridge game. Have three pairs of children extending arms raised above their heads to form three houses with peaked roofs. Some children are wolves and the rest are pigs. The "wolves" blow on the houses as the "pigs" pass through. When the first verse is over, the children forming the straw house lower their arms to catch the child between them as the house "falls down." This pig is sent to stand with the wolves as they "eat him up." At the end of the third verse, the stick house falls and the pig is eaten. At the end of the fifth verse the brick house does not fall and all the remaining pigs run after wolves to tag them. Those caught while you sing the last verse become pigs and play resumes.

Blow the piggy's straw house down,
straw house down,
straw house down.
Blow the piggy's straw house down.
Down it tumbles!

Take the pig and eat him up,
eat him up,
eat him up.
Take the pig and eat him up.
Yum yum juicy!

Blow the piggy's stick house down,
stick house down,
stick house down.
Blow the piggy's stick house down.
Down it tumbles!

Take the pig and eat him up,
eat him up,
eat him up.
Take the pig and eat him up.
Yum yum juicy!

Blow the piggy's brick house down,
brick house down,
brick house down.
Blow the piggy's brick house down.
Uh oh wolfie!

Take the wolf and cook him up,
cook him up,
cook him up.
Take the wolf and cook him up.
Yum yum wolfie!

Pig Pig Wolf Game

This is a variation of the traditional "Duck Duck Goose" tag game.

The leader asks the children to sit on the floor in a circle. The leader walks around the outside of the circle and taps each child on the head. With each tap, the leader says "pig, pig." Then the leader taps a child and says "wolf!" The "wolf" child jumps up and runs around the circle and tries to get back to the empty space before the leader catches her or him. The last one back to the empty space becomes the leader and gets to name the "pig, pig, wolf" on the next round.

Related Skit

Invite the Family

Characters:

> three pigs
> wolf
> more pigs

Plot: Mother Pig sends the three pigs out to live in the world. The pigs build three houses, one from straw, one from sticks, and another from bricks. The wolf blows down the straw and stick houses. The pigs run away and live in the brick house. The wolf can't blow that house down and goes away. When the third pig writes Mama Pig to tell her about his safe brick house, she decides to move the rest of the family in, too. Everyone comes—grandparents, aunts, uncles, and cousins.

Note: In this skit, the children know the basic storyline, and they create their own lines of dialogue as they think the characters might say them.

Simple props and costumes will add interest to the presentation. Cut house shapes out of large cardboard boxes and decorate to look like straw, sticks, or bricks. Children hold the houses up until the wolf blows them down.

For pigs' costumes, cut out pig ears and attach them to a headband. Cut out round, pink circles for snouts and tape them to children's noses. Another kind of snout can be formed with a pink paper cup. Draw the snout on the bottom and punch holes near the lip. Attach an elastic band through the holes to fit around the head so the snout stays on the nose. Cut pink paper spirals for tails.

The wolf costume can be a paperbag mask made from a grocery bag.

Related Three Pigs Activities
(from other Irving and Currie books)

1. "Three Pigs on a Tube," in *Mudluscious* (Libraries Unlimited, 1986), 139-140.

2. "Three Pigs in a Blanket," in *Raising the Roof* (Teacher Ideas Press, 1991), 199-201.

III.
The Three Bears Stories and Activities

Three Bears and Friend

This English folktale about three bears and a young girl named Goldilocks is one of the first stories shared with young children. The bears aren't very scary because they live civilized lives in a house, eating porridge, and sleeping in beds. The traditional story begins as the three bears leave their porridge to cool and go on a walk. In the meantime, a little girl named Goldilocks breaks into their house, samples their porridge, sits in their chairs, and sleeps in Baby Bear's bed.

Repeated sequences in the story delight young children and aid the storyteller. Papa and Mama Bear's porridge is either "too hot" or "too cold" just as their chairs and beds are "too hard" or "too soft." Later in the story, the bears suspect someone has been in the house and ask this series of questions. "Who's been eating my porridge?" "Who's been sitting in my chair?" "Who's been sleeping in my bed?" Each time, the baby bear has a slightly different discovery: his porridge is gone, his chair is broken, and Goldilocks is sleeping in his bed.

Young children remember this sequence with delight, and it is often their first lesson in the structure of folk tales. They learn the number three appears many times—three bears, three bowls of porridge, three chairs, and three beds. Older children can use it to create stories of their own.

This English story appears to have no variants in other cultures, but recent picture books tell the story from other points of view or with variations. James Marshall uses humor in the illustrations for his retelling of *Goldilocks and the Three Bears*. Jan Brett sets *Goldilocks and the Three Bears* in the Ukraine and adds story details in illustrated side panels. Brinton Turkle, in *Deep in the Forest*, reverses the story by having the bear break into the little girl's house. In this book, no words are used, so the children can have the fun of telling the story themselves. Marilyn Tolhurst in *Somebody and the Three Blairs* also uses reversal and word play as the human family, the Blairs, find havoc in their house created by a bear.

Our traditional retelling actually extends the story by having Goldilocks go back to the bears and make amends. Stories, rhymes and songs let children replay the story many times.

Booklist

Barton, Byron. *The Three Bears*. HarperCollins, 1991.

Barton retells the traditional story with a slight variation. Papa Bear's rocker rocks too fast, Mama's is too slow, and Baby Bear's is just right. Bold colors and simple shapes make this picture book an appropriate first version to share.

Brett, Jan. *Goldilocks and the Three Bears*. Dodd, Mead, 1987.

In this version, lavish, detailed illustrations include bears carved into the headboards on beds and embroidered Ukrainian clothes for the bears and Goldilocks. Decorated side panels expand the traditional text. Slightly older children will appreciate this setting.

DeLuise, Dom. *Goldilocks*. Illustrated by Christopher Santoro. Simon & Schuster, 1992.

In this humorous retelling Goldilocks is vain and spoiled. She goes into the woods instead of doing her homework, eats the Bears' soup (pasta e fagioli), sits on the chairs, and tests the beds as in the traditional tale. In the end she apologizes for her behavior, stays for lunch, and no longer disobeys her parents.

Edens, Cooper. *Goldilocks and the Three Bears*. Green Tiger Press, 1989.

Edens provides an historical note and selects forty-six historic illustrations by classic children's book illustrators, including Walter Crane, L. Leslie Brooks, Arthur Rackham, and Jessie Wilcox Smith, to present the traditional tale.

Galdone, Paul. *The Three Bears*. Clarion, 1972.

Galdone's large-scale, humorous illustrations tell the traditional story of the Three Bears and Goldilocks. The text provides explanation for the Bears' lines "Somebody has been sitting in my chair," because "Goldilocks had left the cushion crooked in the chair of the Great Big Bear," and "had squashed down the cushion in the chair of the Middle-Sized Bear." This is a good choice for reading to a large group.

Ives, Penny. *Goldilocks and the Three Bears: A Peek-Through-the-Window Book*. Putnam's, 1992.

In this traditional retelling, die-cut windows reveal small details that expand the story. In one scene of the Bears' kitchen, the reader sees Goldilocks outside the window.

Langley, Jonathan. *Goldilocks and the Three Bears*. HarperCollins, 1991.

The three bears are named George, Mavis, and Brian in this version. Father Bear does the porridge cooking and Mama Bear fixes the Baby's chair with her own hand drill. There is a clever use of different type sizes to indicate the different voices of the bears as they discover Goldilocks has eaten the porridge, sat in their chairs and slept in their beds.

Marshall, James. *Goldilocks and the Three Bears*. Dial, 1988.

Marshall updates the traditional tale with his slightly irreverent touches. The reader is forewarned on the first page that Goldilocks may be capable of mischief as one neighbor declares she is a sweet child, and the other neighbor adds, "That's what you think." Baby Bear's response to his scalding porridge is "Patooie!" and his comment on the broken chair, "broken ... to smithereens" adds a distinctly modern child's reaction. Children who think they are too old for the bears will find Marshall's version fun.

Tolhurst, Marilyn. *Somebody and the Three Blairs*. Illustrated by Simone Abel. Orchard, 1990.
When Mr. and Mrs. Blair and Baby Blair go for a walk, a bear named Somebody comes to visit. He eats their food, sits in their chairs, plays games, and sleeps in their beds. The Blairs discover the bear's havoc, but in the end he escapes.

Turkle, Brinton. *Deep in the Forest*. Dutton, 1976.
In this wordless picture book the story is reversed. A small bear breaks into a log cabin and creates havoc—trying the beds, shaking out feathers from the pillows, tasting the porridge, and breaking chairs. The pioneer family returns and chases out the culprit, who returns to his mama. Children will follow the storyline and be able to retell the story in their own words.

Watts, Bernadette. *Goldilocks and the Three Bears*. North-South Books, 1984.
Originally published in German, the clothes and house depicted in this version have a rural German look. Goldilocks enters the bears' house uninvited and eats porridge, sits in their chairs and finally sleeps in their beds. When the bears come home Goldilocks runs away and never goes back again.

Traditional Story with Media Enhancement

Tell this updated version of "The Three Bears" in which Goldilocks comes back to make amends for her sloppy habits.

You will need pieces of felt to make the following objects: a small cottage, several pine trees to represent the forest, three bowls, muffins, Papa's chair, Mama's chair, Baby's chair—one broken, one fixed—Papa's bed, Mama's bed, Baby's bed, and a sampler that reads "Home Sweet Home." See the patterns on pages 31 and 32. Place these felt pieces on the flannelboard as the story directs.

The Three Bears Retold or Happily Ever After

Once upon a time there lived three bears—Papa Bear, Mama Bear, and Baby Bear. And, you probably know, the three bears lived in a wee little cottage in the middle of a forest. One day, Mama Bear made porridge for breakfast, but it was too hot to eat right away. So, the Bear Family went for a walk in the woods.

Now, while the bears were gone, a little girl whose name was Goldilocks was walking in the woods. She saw the house of the three bears and went right in. She tasted the three bowls of porridge. And, because she liked Baby Bear's porridge best, she ate it all up. She sat in Papa Bear's chair. She sat in Mama Bear's chair. And she sat in Baby Bear's chair. But, Goldilocks was too big for that chair, and she broke it into smithereens. Then, she went upstairs and tried out Papa Bear's bed, Mama Bear's bed, and Baby Bear's bed. And she fell sound asleep in that little bed.

When the bears came home and found the empty cereal bowl, the broken chair, and the messed-up bed, they were furious! They chased Goldilocks out of their house. She didn't come back for a very long time.

But one day, when she was older and wiser, Goldilocks decided to go back into the forest and set things straight. She was ready to make amends, but she wasn't eager to meet the three bears face to face, so she watched and waited until they took another one of their long walks.

One bright sunny morning Mama Bear packed a picnic basket, and Papa Bear and Mama Bear and Baby Bear went into the forest for a picnic lunch. While they were gone, Goldilocks went into the wee little cottage.

Goldilocks saw the bears' three bowls on the table. She made fresh porridge for them to have when they got home for supper. Then she made them three big blueberry muffins as a special treat.

Next, Goldilocks went into the living room. There was Papa Bear's chair and Mama Bear's chair and the broken-up chair of Baby Bear. Goldilocks got out her tool kit, and she hammered and nailed and she fixed that little chair until it looked as good as new. Then she put a little pillow on the chair as a special touch.

Finally, Goldilocks climbed the stairs to the bedrooms. She smoothed out the wrinkles in Papa Bear's bed. She fluffed up the pillows on Mama Bear's bed. And she pulled up the sheets and carefully made Baby Bear's bed. And as an extra special gift, she made a little picture to hang over Baby Bear's bed. Then she hurried home!

In a little while the bears came home from their picnic. They went into their wee little cottage and into the kitchen. They saw the food on the table.

"Who's been cooking in this kitchen?" said Papa Bear.

"Who made these muffins?" said Mama Bear.

"I think I know," said Baby Bear, and he ate up all of his porridge and his blueberry muffin.

Next, the bears went into the living room. They saw the three chairs.

"Who's been working in this living room?" said Papa Bear.

"Who fixed Baby Bear's chair?" said Mama Bear.

"I think I know," said Baby Bear, and he sat right down on his soft pillow in the chair.

Then the three bears went upstairs to their bedrooms.

"Who's been fussing about in this bedroom?" said Papa Bear.

"Who's been straightening this bed?" said Mama Bear.

"I think I know," said Baby Bear, "And she left me a present, too!"

And sure enough, there above Baby Bear's bed was a little cross-stitched sampler that read, "Home Sweet Home." And, in the corner, in very very small stitches, so small that only Baby Bear could actually read them, were the words, "With love to Baby Bear from his friend, Goldilocks."

Goldilocks never went back into the forest again, but the three bears felt much more kindly toward her after that. And you may be sure that everyone, at last, lived happily ever after in the forest.

Big Red and the Bears

(new story version)

Once upon a time there were three bears who lived in a big oak tree in the forest. Now don't get the idea these were uncivilized bears. They had a den, a kitchen, and a bedroom—all with oak paneling.

One morning Mama Bear made flapjacks for breakfast, but she didn't have any honey to put on top.

"Where's my honey?" growled Papa Bear.

"I'm right here, Daddy," said Baby Bear.

"Honey for my flapjacks!" growled Papa Bear.

"Oh, don't be such a grumpy old bear," said Mama Bear. "Let's just go get some."

So Papa Bear, Mama Bear, and Baby Bear set off into the forest to find a beehive. Papa Bear got stung on the tip of his nose, which didn't improve his grumpy disposition. Baby Bear got honey all over his paws, but he had a delicious snack before he started home. Mama Bear collected a whole jar of honey and then some to take back.

As the Bears lumbered back to their old oak tree, they saw a man wearing a red stocking cap and a plaid shirt. He carried a big ax and was looking at their tree.

"Who's that looking at our tree?" said Papa Bear.

"Who's that looking at our tree?" asked Mama Bear.

"Look at that great stocking cap he's got on!" said Baby Bear.

Papa Bear wasn't looking at the man's stocking cap. He was looking at the big ax the man was carrying.

"What's he doing with that ax?" growled Papa Bear.

"What's he doing with ax?" asked Mama Bear.

"Look at that great stocking cap he's got on!" said Baby Bear.

Mama Bear wasn't looking at the man's stocking cap. She knew an ax was used to cut down trees.

The three bears went over to the man.

"Hi," said Papa Bear. "Who are you and what are you doing?"

Big Red said, "I'm Big Red the lumberjack. "There's no timber I can't lumber, and I'm looking at this tree. Sure would make a mighty fine log cabin."

Baby Bear said, "That's our home!"

Mama Bear said, "Why don't you join us for breakfast?"

And Papa Bear said, "Come on inside."

So the three bears and Big Red went into the kitchen. There Big Red saw the stacks of flapjacks. First he saw Baby Bear's eeny, teeny, stack of flapjacks. "This is too small," said Big Red.

Then he saw Mama Bear's stack of flapjacks. "Yuck!" said Big Red. "These have blueberries in them. I can't stand blueberries!"

Then Big Red saw Papa Bear's great, big, stack of flapjacks, and the huge pot of honey Mama had brought home. "Now that's just right!" he said. And in no time at all he had wolfed down every one.

So after breakfast (even though Papa Bear's stomach was still growling), they took Big Red into the den. "Have a seat," said Papa Bear. Big Red looked at the eeny, teeny, chair of Baby Bear. "Too small!" said Big Red. And he looked at Mama Bear's French Provincial chair. "No way!" said Big Red. "I don't speak French!"

Then Big Red saw Papa Bear's recliner. "Ahhhh!" said Big Red as he made himself comfortable. "This is just my size."

But just as he was getting completely relaxed, Baby Bear said, "You're not going to cut down our tree, are you?"

"Suffering saplings," shouted Big Red. "That's why I came to the forest. Where's my ax?" And they all went outside.

Big Red picked up his ax and began to swing it at the tree.

"Wait," called Mama Bear, "Let's cool off for a while. I'll get some lemonade."

So Big Red put down the ax. He saw that Baby Bear was sitting in the sandbox. "Too small!" said Big Red, "and I hate to get sand in my boots."

Then he saw the porch swing for Mama Bear. "Not for me!" said Big Red, "I get dizzy on swings.

Then Big Red saw Papa Bear's hammock. "Perfect!" shouted Big Red, and he made himself comfortable on the hammock. Papa Bear stood beside him. They both looked up at the tree. Way, way, way up at the tree.

"You know," said Papa Bear, "this is a big tree. I wouldn't be surprised if we could get enough lumber for two log cabins out of this tree."

"Now we're barking up the right tree!" said Big Red. "That's just what we can do."

And that's just what they did. With Papa Bear's chainsaw they cut the tree down much faster than Big Red could have with his ax. Then everyone helped raise the roof on two log cabins in the woods. One was for the Bear family. And one was for Big Red.

One morning, Mama Bear made flapjacks and invited Big Red for breakfast. But she didn't have any honey to put on top.

"Where's my honey?" growled Papa Bear.

"I'm right here, Daddy," said Baby Bear.

"Honey for my flapjacks!" growled Papa Bear.

"Oh don't be such a grumpy old bear," said Mama Bear. "Let's just go get some."

So when Big Red arrived, they all set out to find a beehive.

As soon as they were out of sight, a little girl with long, golden curls appeared at the cabin of the three bears. But that's another story!

Literature Enrichment Activities

Writing Activity

Un-BEAR-ably Funny!

Kids love jokes and riddles, especially when they make them up themselves. No matter how silly, they will laugh. Even reluctant readers can sometimes be convinced to find out the answers to riddles. Encourage children to use rhyme and word-play to write jokes, riddles, and tongue-twisters. And don't forget knock-knock jokes!

Here are some samples.

Knock-knock.
Who's there?
Bet
Bet who?
Bet you don't know who ate all my porridge.

Tongue twister: Brown bears bring brimming bowls of blueberries for breakfast.

Q: When the bears go walking in the forest, what kind of shoes do they wear?
A: None. They go bear-footed.

Speaking Activities

Goldilocks Or: What Happens to People Who Do Not Remember Their Manners
(Tune: "Three Blind Mice")

Goldilocks
In the woods
Doesn't do
What she should
She entered the house of three happy bears
They went out a-walking, but she didn't care!
She opened the door and went up the stairs.
Goldilocks, Goldilocks.

Goldilocks,
In the house
Much much worse
Than a mouse.
She tasted the porridge of Papa Bear.
She sat in the Mama's most cozy chair
And slept in the bed till they found her there!
Goldilocks, Goldilocks.

Goldilocks,
Woke right up,
Saw those bears,
Made a fuss.
The bears heard her holler as she ran out.
Then Papa Bear said, "What's that all about?
Well, she's learned her lesson, without a doubt."
Goldilocks, Goldilocks.

Meet the Bears
(action rhyme)

Papa bear was very tall,
      (Reach high.)
With a big bear voice.
      (Cup hands around mouth.)
He had a green bowl,
      (Make a large circle with hands.)
and a big hard chair,
      (Pat chair firmly.)
and he slept in a great big bed.
      (Rest head on hand. Snore.)
ZZZZZZZ....

Mama Bear liked to sing a song
      (Hold up hands shoulder high.)
in a happy Mama Bear voice.
      (Wiggle fingers by mouth.)
She had a yellow bowl
      (Make medium circle with hands.)
and a soft comfy chair
      (Pat chair softly.)
and she slept in a downy feather bed
      (Rest head on hands. Sing.)
Lalalalalalala

Baby Bear was not very big
      (Hold hand low to ground.)
but he sure got good bear hugs
      (Hug self.)
He had a red bowl
      (Make small bowl with hands.)
and a wee tiny chair
      (Pat chair lightly.)
and a bed just baby bear size
      (Rest head on hands. Sigh.)
MMMMM-MMMM.

Goldi's Song
(Tune: "My Bonnie Lies Over the Ocean")

I'm wandering out in the forest
I'm here in the woods all alone
But look up ahead there's a cottage
It looks like nobody is home.
Should I go in
Or should I just run away, away
I'll just peek in
Then decide if I should stay.
I'm running out fast from the forest
I've come nose to nose with the bears
I've learned not to break into houses
I really have had quite a scare.
Running Running
Out of the forest and through the woods
I'll remember
Next time I know I'll be good.

Related Craft

Three Bears Diorama

Using the diorama background (page 38) and the characters of the three bears (below), cut out on solid lines and fold on dotted lines. Cut the slits in the scene to insert the characters. Tape side b to tab a to make the scene of the three bears' home stand up for you.

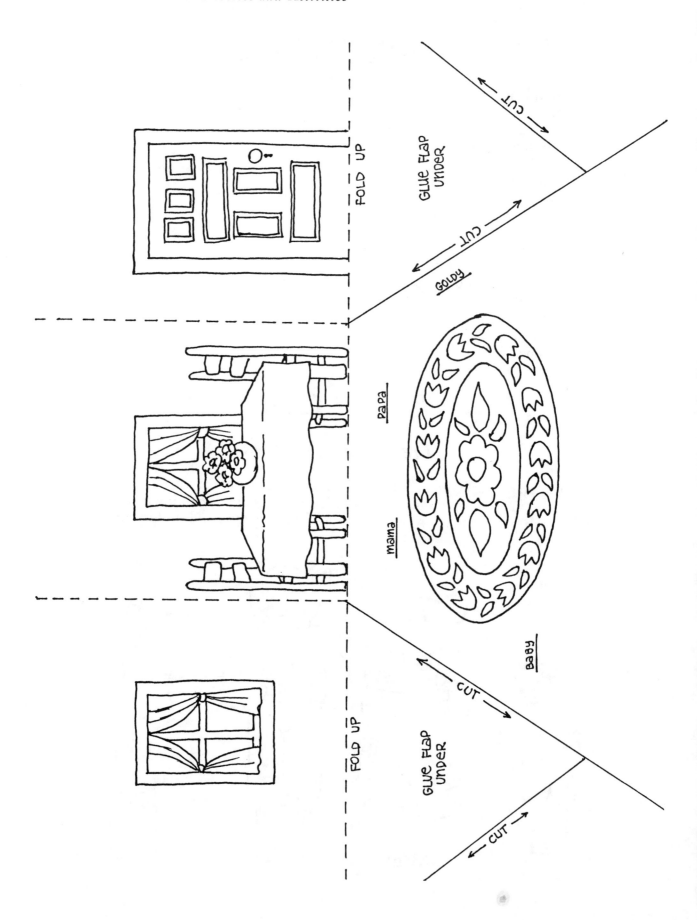

Related Game

Mama Bear Says

This is a variation of "Simon says," the kind of game that helps children listen for directions. The leader begins by instructing the children to perform an action only when the statement is preceded by "Mama Bear says...." Use the following dialogue as an example.

Leader: Little bears like to have a lot of fun, but sometimes Mama Bear has to remind them by saying "Mama Bear says stand up."
(Children stand up.)
"Mama Bear says run in place."
(Children run in place)
Jump three times. Oops!
Mama Bear didn't say that.
(Children hold still.)
Now, Mama Bear says jump three times. Good.
(Children jump.)

(Continue in this manner.)

Related Skit

Don't Go In!

Characters:

　　Papa Bear
　　Mama Bear
　　Baby Bear
　　Goldilocks
　　trees in forest (as many as you like)
　　other forest animals if desired

Plot: The Bears leave their breakfast on the table and go for a walk. Goldilocks comes through the woods. The trees and animals warn her not to go into the forest any further, and not to go into the Bears' house. Goldilocks does anyway. She eats their breakfast, sits in their chairs, tries their beds, and falls asleep. Back in the forest the trees and animals tell the Bears to go home. Led by the chatter of the animals and a forest brigade, the Bears express horror at the mess inside their house. The trees point out a sleeping Goldilocks upstairs. The Bears demand an explanation from her. Sheepishly, she makes an excuse that she got lost in the woods, came inside but didn't mean to leave the mess. The Bears show her to the door as the forest animals help her find her way home. The trees hold up a sign that reads "And don't come back!"

Notes: In this skit, the children know the basic storyline and they create their own lines of dialogue as they think the characters might say them.

Simple props and costumes will add interest to the presentation. The Bears can wear brown paper-bag masks with paper-ear cutouts. Goldilocks' mask can have yellow yarn hair. The trees can have green tissue paper stuck to the top of the masks for leaves. Forest animals can have paper plate masks and paper tails pinned to their clothes.

Related Three Bears Activity
(from another Irving and Currie book)

1. "Knock, Knock Who's There?" in *Raising the Roof* (Teacher Ideas Press, 1991), 196-197.

IV.
The Frog Prince Stories and Activities

Some Day Your Frog Will Come

The two major themes of this tale are the importance of keeping promises, and the potential for transformation in all of us. When the princess loses her ball in a pond, a frog offers to get it if she will let him be her companion at the castle. She promises freely, but as soon as the ball is retrieved, she runs home. The frog follows but the princess tries valiantly to ignore him. Her father insists that a princess should keep her promise. Reluctantly the girl lets the frog eat with her and allows him to go to the bedroom. Upon the frog's insistence, she kisses him whereupon the spell is broken and the frog becomes a prince.

This folktale has been retold in numerous picture books. Several versions add humor to the story, imagining the frog unhappy with his lot as a prince. It may be that the prince is not as handsome as expected, or maybe the princess is just not worth the trouble. Rachel Isadora's *The Princess and the Frog* and Paul Galdone's *The Frog Prince* are picture book versions that feature a traditional retelling. Fred Gwynne's new version, *Pondlarker*, and Jon Scieszka's *The Frog Prince Continued* both tell the story of what happens to the frog prince after the magic transformation.

Princess Pug in our story is less haughty and willing to accept less than perfection. There are many opportunities to play the part of the frog or write newspaper accounts of the wedding. This story lends itself well to contemporary retellings. It is not frightening, and it points out that things are never what they seem.

Booklist

Berenzy, Alix. *A Frog Prince*. Henry Holt, 1989.
This lavishly illustrated retelling of the traditional tale adds new twists. The frog is sent out to perform brave deeds so he can kiss the human princess and be restored to his handsome self. He really is put off by the princess' spoiled ways, and when he finds a castle with a beautiful frog princess sleeping inside, he decides to remain a frog and rule the kingdom with her.

Grimm, Jacob, and Wilhelm Grimm. *The Frog Prince*. Illustrated by Robert Baxter. Troll, 1979.

This traditional telling of the story emphasizes the promise that the princess has to keep. The princess cooperates to a point, but then in disgust, throws the frog against the wall. He is restored to his princely self, grateful and ready to live happily ever after.

Grimm, Jacob, and Wilhelm Grimm. *The Frog Prince*. Illustrated by Paul Galdone. McGraw-Hill, 1974.

Paul Galdone's humorous pictures show the frog as green and lumpy, warts and all. The princess must obey the king and be true to her word. She throws the frog against the wall to turn him into a prince. There is an infrequently used ending where Henry, the servant of the prince, has had his heart bound by iron bars to keep it from breaking when the prince was put under the witch's spell. He now bursts the bands with joy at the prince's happiness.

Grimm, Jacob, and Wilhelm Grimm. *The Frog Prince or Iron Henry*. Illustrated by Binette Schroeder. North-South Books, 1989.

The text for this book is from the original 1812 edition of tales by the Grimm brothers. Originally published in Germany, the traditional tale of the frog who is transformed into a prince has an additional character. Henry, the prince's servant, was so sad when a witch put a spell on his master and changed him into a frog, that Henry wore three iron bands around his chest to keep his heart from breaking. As the prince and princess drive away the bands on the servant break off and Henry rejoices to have his prince back. The illustrations are striking with a variety of points of view and the text placed in unusual areas on the page. The visual transformation of the frog into the prince is particularly striking.

Gwynne, Fred. *Pondlarker*. Simon & Schuster, 1990.

Because his mother has read him the story of the frog prince, Pondlarker decides to go find a princess. When he does, she is old so he changes his mind. Pondlarker returns to the pond to raise a large family of frogs.

Isadora, Rachel. *The Princess and the Frog*. Greenwillow, 1989.

Watercolor paintings tell the story of the princess who promises a frog he can come to the palace if he will retrieve her ball. The frog stays three nights at the palace before he becomes a handsome prince.

Ormerod, Jan. *The Frog Prince*. Lothrop, Lee & Shepard, 1990.

In this version, the Queen insists the princess keep her promise to the frog. After the princess sleeps with the frog three nights and grows to love him, he turns into a prince.

Scieszka, Jon. *The Frog Prince Continued*. Illustrated by Steve Johnson. Viking, 1991.

In this sequel to the traditional story, the princess and frog prince are miserable, so the frog prince tries to find someone to turn him back into a frog. He meets three witches from traditional fairy tales who cause him to escape into the woods, where he meets a fairy godmother inexperienced in frog spells. He turns into a carriage before turning back into the frog prince. Finally, he kisses the princess when the two become frogs.

Tarcov, Edith. *The Frog Prince*. Illustrated by James Marshall. Scholastic, 1974.

This retelling of the Princess who must keep her promises to a frog is part of the Hello Reading series. It is written at Reading Level 3 for Grades 1 and 2. The story is fun to read and includes sound effects and a rhyme the frog croaks to remind the princess of her promise. The facial expressions in the illustrations add to the fun.

Vesey, A. *The Princess and the Frog*. Puffin, 1988.

When the princess brings a frog who has found her ball back to the palace, the Queen hopes that the frog might be a prince in disguise. The animal is treated like a prince, but he never turns into one. He refuses to leave the palace, and even moves in his family of little frogs.

Traditional Story with Media Enhancement

Use old socks to make the two-sided puppet of the frog prince as shown in the diagram on page 45. Use a princess puppet, or put on a crown and play the part of the princess yourself.

The Frog Prince Retold

Once there was a beautiful princess who had a favorite golden ball. As she was tossing it in the air one day, it landed smack in the middle of a pond. She cried so loudly that a frog on a nearby lily pad jumped over to ask her,

"Why are you crying, Princess?"

"I've lost my beautiful golden ball in the pond."

"Stop crying. I can get your ball."

"You can?"

"Certainly. But, what will you give me in return?"

"I could give you my pearls. Or my crown."

"What would I do with those?" said the frog.

"Well, what do you want?"

The frog looked at the princess. "What I want is to come to your palace and eat at your table and sleep in your bed."

The princess did not want to let him do any of those things, but she would promise anything to get her ball back. So she said, "Yes, of course you may. Just please get my ball."

The frog jumped into the pond, and in seconds, he flipped the ball back to the princess. Immediately, she took off running for the palace, leaving the frog behind.

The frog had to squish and slip all the way to the palace on his own. But he finally made it and knocked on the door.

The princess ran to the door but when she saw it was the frog, she slammed the door in his face. Her father, the king asked, "Who was at the door?"

The princess answered, "Just a frog I met today. He got my golden ball out of the pond, and I promised him he could come to the palace for dinner."

"Then you must let him in. A promise is a promise," said the king.

So the princess let the frog in. He jumped into the dining room and sat on the table to eat. He did not have very good manners, and the princess could hardly eat for watching him. Finally dinner was over.

"Now," said the frog, "it's time for bed."

The princess did not want the frog on her lovely bed, but the king reminded her, "A promise is a promise." And she led him upstairs.

The princess lay down in bed. The frog hopped in beside her and asked for a goodnight kiss. "Yech," thought the princess. "I can't kiss a frog." But she did what she could. She blew him a kiss.

Well, that kiss knocked the frog off the bed, and when the princess looked over the end, she saw a handsome prince where the frog had been!

The frog, who was now a prince, said, "I was under a spell that could only be broken by the kiss of a princess. Marry me."

So the very next day the princess and the frog prince were married and lived happily ever after.

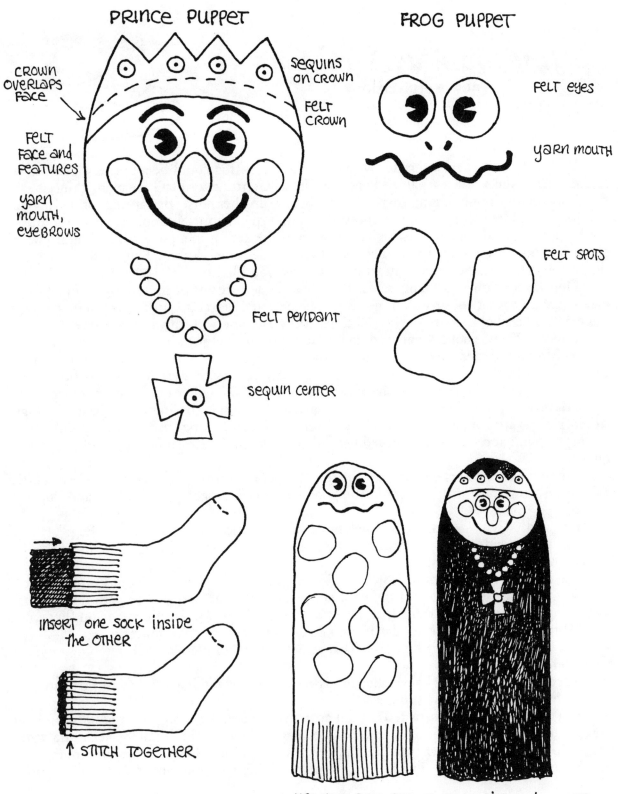

PRINCE PUPPET

FROG PUPPET

CROWN OVERLAPS FACE

SEQUINS ON CROWN

FELT CROWN

FELT FACE and FEATURES

yarn MOUTH, EYEBROWS

FELT eyes

yarn mouth

FELT SPOTS

FELT PENDANT

SEQUIN CENTER

INSERT one sock inside the OTHER

↑ STITCH TOGETHER

USE HOT GLUE GUN TO STICK PIECES TO SOCKS

Just the Way You Are
(new story version)

Back at a time when wishes really mattered and any frog could be a prince waiting to be kissed, there lived a princess named Penelope Ursula Gertrude, or PUG for short. Princess Pug didn't spend much time kissing frogs. She was busy riding her horse, or dancing, or playing her lute for the children of the village. Princess Pug didn't spend hours in front of the mirror brushing her long golden hair, because it was brown and she kept it in a ponytail. She didn't worry about spoiling her lovely dresses because she wore sensible clothes. She didn't wear glass slippers, either, because everybody knows they give you blisters.

One day her father, the king, said, "Pug, dear, I don't see any princes lining up outside the palace gate to ask for your hand in marriage. Maybe you'd better go out to the pond and see if there are some frogs to kiss. Maybe you'll get lucky and one will turn into a prince."

Princess Pug was not all that crazy to find a prince, but some of her best friends were frogs so she didn't mind spending some time kissing them. She kissed one frog and it turned into a cow. "Wrong spell," she said. She kissed a second one, and it grew wings and flew away. "Oops," said Pug, The third frog she kissed disappeared altogether in a puff of smoke.

Princess Pug saw there was only one frog left. He wasn't the most handsome of frogs, either. He was kind of pale green and he had very big feet for a frog. But he was the only thing left in the pond and Pug had promised her father to try, so she closed her eyes and gave him a big smack.

When she opened her eyes she saw the frog had indeed turned into a prince. He was a little pale, but sitting there with his feet in the pool, he looked altogether acceptable and Pug was pleased.

Pug said, "Hello, My name is Penelope Ursula Gertrude. You can call me Pug."

The prince said "Hello. I'm Prince Gilbert. You can call me Gil." Pug was relieved that he didn't croak when he talked.

Pug said, "So you're a prince after all. Father will be so glad to meet you. Come on out."

So the prince stepped out of the pool and stood up. That's when they both noticed that something of the prince's past life had stayed with him. His feet were still green and flippered.

"Hmmm," said Pug. "I wonder if the kiss takes time to work completely."

The prince looked at his flippers. "That appears to be all the magic we're going to get. I hope you don't mind."

Since Pug didn't really know what to expect and she really liked Gil from the start, she said, "I like you just the way you are."

So Pug and Gil were married. They led an active life together. Pug rode her horse and Gil taught her to play water polo. Pug taught him how to dance and Gil taught her to do water ballet. Pug wasn't very good at track and field events at first, but Gil was a natural jumper and a patient teacher. Before long, Pug learned to jump hurdles with Gil, and they lived "hoppily" ever after.

Literature Enrichment Activities
Writing Activity

Up to the Minute

Write articles for a class newspaper, interviewing various characters in the Frog Prince story. Ask the princess if she expected such a handsome prince? Ask other frogs how they feel about a frog who's made good? Ask the palace cook if he has to put flies in the soup?

The newspaper can carry pages on the wedding fashion, home improvement hints for fixing up the pad, advice column, and frog sports. Maybe a medical advice column could suggest ways to get rid of a frog in the throat!

Speaking Activities

Glad to Be a Frog
(Tune: "If You're Happy and You Know It")

I'm so glad to be a bull frog on a pond
I'm so glad to be a bull frog on a pond
I'm so glad to be a frog, rollin' carefree off a log
I'm so glad to be a bull frog on a pond

I don't want to be a prince and wear a crown
I don't want to be a prince and wear a crown
I don't want to be a prince, that would surely make me wince
I don't want to be a prince and wear a crown

I would rather croak and eat up bugs and flies
I would rather croak and eat up bugs and flies
I would dine on bugs and flies up until the day I die
I would rather croak and eat up bugs and flies

A proper prince must act so mannerly
A proper prince must act so mannerly
For a prince must eat his peas and remember to say "please"
A proper prince must act so mannerly

I would rather be a frog so I can burp
I would rather be a frog so I can burp
Let me gulp up all I please, make a burp down to my knees!
I'd rather be a frog so I can burp!

What's Inside?
(action rhyme)

There's a big bull frog
    (Sit with legs folded, hands on knees.)
With two bulgy eyes
    (Circle eyes with fingers.)
And a long, long tongue
    (Stick out tongue.)
For catching flies.
    (Clap several times in air.)
If I had green skin
    (Point to skin.)
I'd run and hide
    (Hide face in hands.)
Maybe he thinks
    (Point to head.)
He's a prince inside
    (Bow.)

Splash! Squish! Smack!
(chant)

Use the two-line rhyme to encourage children to brainstorm sounds a frog can make. First make a list of the possible sounds. Then set a rhythm by slapping hands on knees and clapping. Repeat the rhyme and combine sound words to set up as much internal rhyme as you can. For example: splash-crash or glide-slide.

Around the pond and into the lake
Tell me the sounds a frog can make.
Splash, crash.

Around the pond and into the lake
Tell me the sounds a frog can make.
Splash, crash.
Glide, slide.

Related Crafts

Shoes Fit for a Frog Prince

Give each child a copy of the frog prince shoe pattern on page 49 to decorate appropriately for a frog prince.

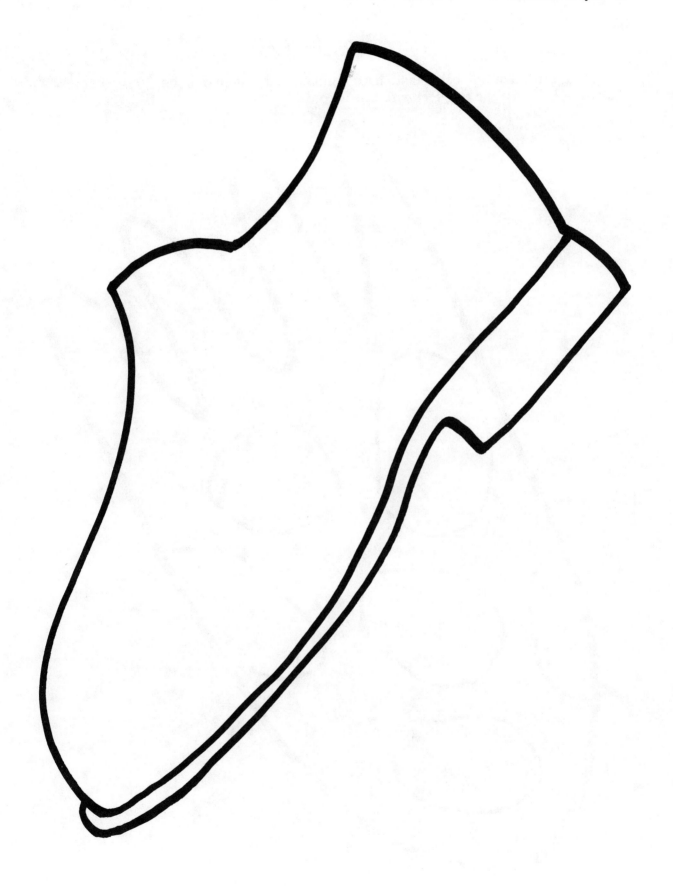

Frog Feet

Enlarge the pattern below and have children trace around it on green, light-weight posterboard. Attach the frog feet with elastic cord.

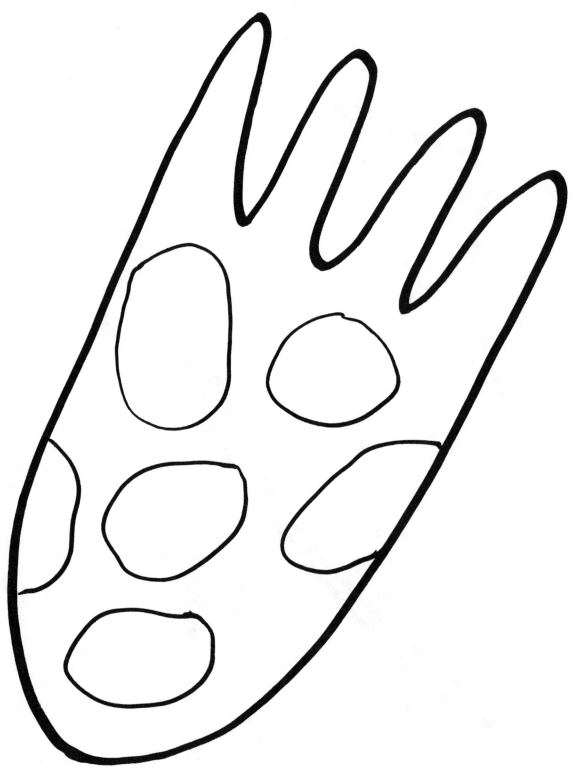

Related Game

Pass It On

Use an orange for the princess' gold ball. Teams must pass the ball as a frog would, without using their hands or mouths. The ball is passed and received under the chin. The first team to pass the ball all the way to the end wins fish crackers for hungry frogs.

Related Skit

Don't Want a Prince

Characters:

> princess
> princes
> frogs

Plot: All the eligible princes in the nearby kingdoms come to a ball at the palace. After dancing with them, the princess escapes to the garden. She would rather play with the frogs in the pond than marry any of the princes. One frog tells her he's really a prince under the green skin. The princess tells him she doesn't want a prince. She plays leap-frog and sings choruses down at the pond the rest of her days.

Note: In this skit, suggest this basic storyline to the children and guide them in creating their own lines of dialogue as they think the characters might say them.

Simple props and costumes will add interest to the presentation. Make paper crowns for the princes and the princess. Using the pattern on page 50, make frog feet for all of the frogs.

Related Frog Prince Activity
(from another Irving and Currie book)

1. "Prince-less Princess Or Mind Your Manners with a Frog," in *Glad Rags* (Libraries Unlimited, 1987), 130-132.

V.
Cinderella
Stories
and Activities

I'd Never Recognize You in Those Glad Rags

The Cinderella story is one of the oldest in the world and the most cross-cultural. More than 200 versions have originated in places as diverse as Egypt and Vietnam, France, and the United States. The basic story involves a girl who is orphaned or set apart from society and is given help from a magic source. She attends a ball or celebration, loses an important object (usually a shoe), is sought after by a prince or ruler. The girl demonstrates worthiness by being hard working, kind, or at least persistent. She usually has small feet, perhaps showing the influence from the Chinese culture of foot binding. The transformation theme from rags to riches may not be as astonishing as it seems. Earlier European versions held that the "cinder girl" was actually of noble birth to begin with. Still, the change of appearance is a central event in most of the tales.

The Egyptian Cinderella, one of the oldest heroines dating back to the sixth century B.C., wears rose-red slippers. In the Chinese version, Yeh-Shen is helped by a magic fish who gives her golden slippers. Tattercoats from England takes care of geese, is loved in her plain clothes by the Prince, but her clothes are transformed in the end. The rough-faced or scar-faced girl in Algonquin Indian lore becomes disfigured from tending fire. Because she is the only one who can see the Invisible Being, her scars are washed away. Perrault's French version introduces the fairy godmother as the source of magic.

One of the values of sharing the Cinderella story is showing its many cultural roots. Children need to know that Walt Disney didn't write the story, and the French fairy-godmother version isn't the prototype. People all over the world may tell a similar story, but they tell it in their style and with elements particular to their own culture.

Booklist

Climo, Shirley. *The Egyptian Cinderella*. Illustrated by Ruth Heller. HarperCollins, 1989.

Rhodopis is a Greek slave owned by a family in Egypt. Her only joy is a pair of beautiful red slippers. One day a falcon steals one of the shoes and Rhodopis is heartbroken. But the falcon drops the shoe in the lap of Pharaoh, who does not rest until he finds the owner and makes her his queen.

Climo, Shirley. *The Korean Cinderella*. Illustrated by Ruth Heller. HarperCollins, 1993.

A lovely Korean girl, Pear Blossom, is badly treated by her stepmother and stepsister. A magic frog helps Pear Blossom do the tasks her stepmother assigns in time to see the prince in a procession. He sees her lose her sandal and seeks the girl with one shoe to marry. This version includes very real Korean customs and brightly colored drawings that fill the pages.

Cole, Babette. *Prince Cinders*. Putnam's, 1987.

Cole tells a reverse Cinderella with Prince Cinders bothered by his stepbrothers and doing all the work. A little magic changes him into an ape for the big ball where he loses his pants in his haste to leave. The princess uses the pants to track down Prince Cinders and they are married.

Ehrlich, Amy. *Cinderella*. Illustrated by Susan Jeffers. Dial, 1985.

In this retelling of the Perrault story, Cinderella is aided by a fairy godmother so she can attend a royal ball where she meets the Prince. In the end she forgives her stepsisters who join her at the palace. Jeffers' fine pen and ink and watercolor illustrations set a magical mood.

Hooks, William H. *Moss Gown*. Illustrated by Donald Carrick. Clarion, 1987.

This traditional Southern tale combines elements of King Lear and Cinderella. Because her father misunderstands her words, Candace is disinherited and later turned out of the family home by her two older sisters. The banished young woman receives a shimmering moss gown from a witch woman, but is warned that the gown will turn to rags when the morning star fades. Candace then works as a scullery maid and by calling upon the witch woman is able to make her rags turn back into the moss gown so she can attend a ball to meet the master of the house. The story ends as Candace marries and is happily reunited with her father who has come to understand his daughter's words.

Huck, Charlotte. *Princess Furball*. Illustrated by Anita Lobel. Greenwillow, 1989.

In this variant, a princess runs away from home to avoid marriage to an ogre. Hiding her identity, she works as a servant in the castle of a handsome prince. While this Cinderella also meets the prince at a ball, she wins him through her own cleverness without the help of a fairy godmother.

Karlin, Barbara. *Cinderella*. Illustrated by James Marshall. Little, Brown, 1989.

This funny retelling of the traditional story includes a fairy godmother who says "Silly me," as she transforms Cinderella's rags into an elegant gown. The stepsisters wear too much makeup and the prince rests in a hammock. Slightly older children will enjoy these humorous touches.

Louie, Ai-Ling. *Yeh-Shen*. Illustrated by Ed Young. Philomel, 1982.

In this Chinese tale, Yeh-Shen is mistreated by a stepmother, but given golden slippers and fine clothes by a magic fish. Eventually, the king falls in love with her.

Martin, Rafe. *The Rough-Face Girl*. Illustrated by David Shannon. Putnam's, 1992.

In this Algonquin Indian tale, the rough-faced girl is scarred from years of tending the fire for the family. She is mistreated by her sisters, who proudly go off to marry the Invisible Being, but cannot really see him. The rough-faced girl goes in search of the Invisible Being on her own. The sister of the Invisible Being asks certain questions to test the rough-faced girl, but the girl is able to see the Invisible Being as no others could and answers the questions. When she bathes in the lake, her scars vanish and she marries the Invisible Being.

Myers, Bernice. *Sidney Rella and the Glass Sneaker*. Macmillan, 1985.

In this modern version, Sidney Rella wants to play football, and is helped by a fairy god-father who gives him a fancy uniform and a pair of glass sneakers. This new twist to the old tale will appeal especially to older students who can appreciate the humor.

Perrault, Charles. *Cinderella*. Illustrated by Marcia Brown. Macmillan, 1954.

Winner of the Caldecott Medal, the soft line drawings illustrate this magical tale of the cinder girl who, with the help of her fairy godmother, is transformed into a lovely princess and attends a ball. Here she meets the prince and loses her glass slipper in her haste to be home before midnight when the magic ends. The prince traces her through her slipper and they marry.

Perrault, Charles. *Cinderella*. Illustrated by Errol Le Cain. Puffin, 1972.

Le Cain's intricate illustrations add new meaning to the Perrault story. In elaborate borders, the lizard's coat becomes the coat of the footman, and Cinderella's elegant clothes change into rags in a series of five sequenced pictures.

Perrault, Charles. *Cinderella*. Illustrated by Roberto Innocenti. Creative Education, 1983.

Innocenti's sophisticated illustrations set in the 1920s in London add a touch of realism to the traditional text. The final illustration will cause readers to question whether or not Cinderella really lived happily ever after.

Sharto, Russell. *Cinderella: The Untold Story*. Illustrated by Lewis Birch. Lore Press, 1990.

This book is two stories in one. One side has the traditional Cinderella story. Flip the book over and hear the stepsisters' side of the tale!

Steel, Flora Annie. *Tattercoats*. Illustrated by Diane Goode. Bradbury, 1976.

Tattercoats is shunned by her grandfather, and not allowed to attend the king's ball. But a gooseherd plays magical tunes for her, causing the prince to fall in love with the girl, and making her rags turn into shining robes.

Wegman, William. *Cinderella*. With Carole Kismaric and Marvin Heiferman. Hyperion Publishers, 1993.

A traditional retelling of the poor girl whose fairy godmother uses magic to get her to the ball. This book has a hilarious twist: the illustrations are photographs of dogs dressed up in human clothing.

Traditional Story
with Media Enhancement

Draw the lines as indicated in the story on a chalkboard, poster board, or overhead projector.

Cinderella Retold

There once was a lovely girl whose father married a woman with two daughters of her own. The girl was forced to work all day and sleep by the fire at night. She was called Cinderella. Here is where Cinderella lived. (Point to beginning dot.)

One day, an invitation came to all the young ladies of the kingdom to attend a ball at the palace. The prince was going to choose a wife. Cinderella's stepsisters were very excited. Cinderella wanted to go to the ball, too, but the stepmother and sisters kept her so busy getting them ready she had no time to make her own dress. After they left she went into the garden and cried (draw line 1).

Then a voice said, "Why are you crying?"

Cinderella looked up. "I want to go to the ball," she said. Then she asked, "Who are you?"

"I'm your fairy godmother," replied the visitor. "I can make your wishes come true."

So the fairy godmother changed pumpkins to coaches and mice to horses, and gave Cinderella the most beautiful ball gown and tiny glass slippers.

"You must be home by midnight when the spell ends," she called as Cinderella left for the palace (draw line 2).

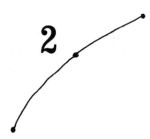

All night the prince and Cinderella danced together. She was the loveliest girl there. Even the stepsisters did not recognize her.

Suddenly the clock began to chime. Bong-bong-bong.

"I have to go," said Cinderella to the prince.

Bong-bong-bong. "Wait," said the prince, "I don't know your name."

Bong-Bong-Bong. As the last chime sounded Cinderella ran to the street and all her magic was gone (draw line 3).

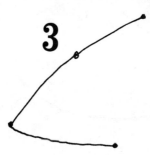

The next day the prince set out to find the lovely girl from the ball. He did not know her name or where she lived. He traveled from house (draw line 4) to house (draw line 5) through the village.

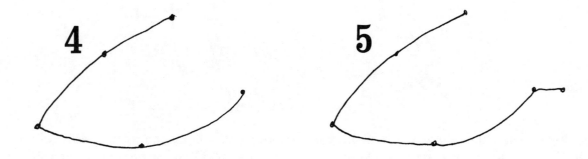

He went to one house (draw line 6) and another (draw line 7), but there was no lovely girl.

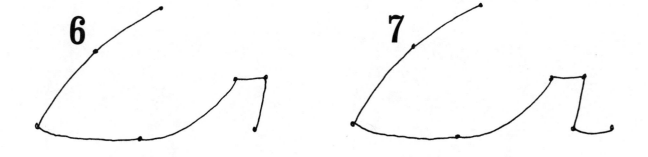

Then he came to the last house in the village (draw line 8), Cinderella's.

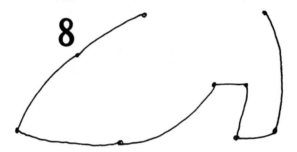

The prince met the stepsisters, but did not think they were pretty enough to be his lost love. On the way out he met Cinderella (draw line 9). She was dirty and her hair was messed from working all day, but the prince thought he saw something about her that was familiar.

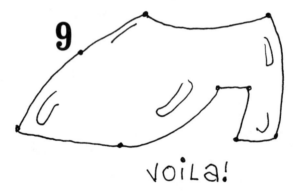

But he knew the one way to tell. He had something that belonged to the beautiful girl, something she dropped at the ball. Do you know what it was? (Drawing will now be of a shoe.) Yes, he had her shoe. He tried it on her and it fit perfectly. They were married and lived happily ever after.

Just Enough Magic
(new story version)

There was once a girl named Cinderella, but everyone called her Ella. She had two sisters who were very lazy. Whenever the beans had to be hoed, or the weeds had to be pulled from the pumpkin patch, Ella got no help at all from her sisters.

One day during the harvest season, the prince decided to have a Harvest Ball. Ella's sisters spent days trying on dresses and doing their hair to go to the ball. Ella wanted to go to the ball, too, because she loved to dance. But just then the corn and the apples and brussels sprouts needing picking. So she did not have time to get a new dress. The sisters left for the ball while Ella was finishing the last row of brussels sprouts. As she heard the carriage drive away she sighed and said, "Well, my feet feel like dancing even if the rest of me isn't ready. At least I'm only stuck in the mud instead of being a wallflower."

"Stuck in the mud! I'm stuck in the mud!" came a voice by Ella's feet.

Ella looked on the ground and there was a wee little wizard, no bigger than a brussels sprout. She pulled him out of the mud and set him in the palm of her hand.

"Thank you very much," he said. "Now, for your kindness, perhaps I can help you."

"Really?" Ella asked.

"Well, actually I'm rather new at this. I'm just a wizard in training. But I'm willing to try if you are."

Ella could see that even a little magic would be better than none at all, so she agreed.

"Great," said the wizard. "First, bring me a brussels sprout so I can make you a coach."

She brought him the brussels sprout and he said the magic words and a coach did appear. Unfortunately it was a coach the size of a brussels sprout.

Ella sighed.

"Wrong color?" asked the wizard. "Oh," he said, "too small."

Ella nodded. "You know," she said, "there is a coach in the carriage house. It needs to be painted and have a wheel fixed, and then it will be fine."

So the wizard said the special words and there was just enough magic to make the coach a bright blue with four gold wheels.

"Great," said Ella.

"Now," said the wizard, "let me change those rags into the grandest ball gown in the world. Turn around three times and it will be ready."

So Ella turned around three times, but her clothes changed into a nightgown. "Flannel might be heavy for the ball," Ella said. "I have a nice dress. All it needs is to be fixed up a little."

So the wizard had just enough magic to add sparkle and lace to Ella's dress to make it special.

"Wonderful," said Ella.

They both looked at her bare feet.

"Glass slippers!" shouted the wizard. "My greatest feat yet!" He said the magic words and glass slippers were on her feet.

"I did it," shouted the wizard.

"These are really very pretty," said Ella, "but I love to dance. These would give me blisters. I really would like a pair of pink ballet slippers, if you don't mind."

"Of course not," said the wizard. He was sure he could do any kind of magic now. He said the words and there were the slippers.

"Be home by midnight when the magic ends," the wizard warned.

The evening went by quickly. Cinderella and the prince danced so well together they knew they were made for each other. But soon the clock began to chime twelve.

Running out of the palace as fast as she could, she lost one pink ballet slipper. The prince found it and vowed to marry the girl it fit.

The next day, Ella was back in coveralls and garden boots. Her sisters could not stop talking about the ball and the wonderful dancer the prince had met. They were still talking when the royal coach drew up in front of the house and the prince stepped out.

"Did either of you lose this slipper at the ball last night," he asked.

"I did," said the first sister.

She crowded her foot into the slipper and began to dance with the prince. She stepped all over his feet.

"No," said the prince. "I didn't dance with you."

"Of course not. I was the one," said the other sister.

She rammed her foot into the slipper. Then she took two dance steps with the prince and fell down.

"No," he said, "You were not the one. Is there anyone else here?"

But the sisters did not even mention Ella.

As the prince got into the royal coach, he decided to ask the gardener if there were any other young girls in the neighborhood. To his surprise the gardener was Ella. Even in her work clothes he saw there was something special about her. He stepped out of the coach into the garden, and handed her the pink ballet slipper. Ella put it on, and then took the mate from her pocket and put it on. She fairly floated into the prince's arms. They waltzed up the rows of squash, they fox-trotted in the cucumbers, and twirled in the beets. The prince had found his bride.

So Ella went off to live happily ever after in the palace. And as for her two sisters, Ella made sure they were never bored or lazy again. She put one in charge of hoeing the beans, and the other one responsible for weeding the pumpkin patch.

Literature Enrichment Activities
Writing Activities

Having a Lovely Time

Extend the story of Cinderella by imagining what kind of postcard she might send on her honeymoon to her stepmother. Give students a plain 4" × 6" file card, and have them draw a picture on one side of the card of the place where Cinderella and the Prince are visiting. On the other side of the card, write an appropriate message and address.

For example, draw a picture of the Sphinx. The message reads:

Dear Stepmother,

The prince and I are having a lovely time here in Egypt. We have found many kings here who seem to be living happily ever after. Please don't expect us back for a long time.

Sincerely,

Cinderella

My Own Fairy Tale

Have children retell Cinderella's story in a different style. For example, write the story as it might have appeared in Cindrella's diary, or the diary of one of the sisters. Another style is to rewrite the story as in a romance magazine. Or write the story as a newspaper announcement for the wedding.

Speaking Activities

Song of the Two Stepsisters
(Tune: "She'll Be Comin' Round the Mountain")

Divide the children into two groups. One group sings the first verse of the first stepsister. The second group sings the second verse of the second stepsister.

First Step Sister:

I am getting ready for the prince's ball
Cinderella's staying home—I guess she'll bawl.
I don't care if she's unhappy
'Cause I think she's really sappy
And for me the prince will surely take a fall.

Second Step Sister:

> I'm the younger sister but I'm first in line.
> At the palace I will dance and I will dine.
> Cinderella may be pretty,
> But she's not so very witty.
> So the prince will say to me, "Won't you be mine?"

At the Ball
(Tune: "My Bonnie Lies Over the Ocean")

Divide the class into two groups. The first group sings Cinderella's part, and the second group sings the part of the prince.

Cinderella sings:

> I don't want to be a wallflower
> I'm here at the dance all alone
> I hope the prince asks me to dance soon
> At midnight I have to go home
> Waiting, hoping,
> When will the prince ever take a chance?
> I'm all dressed up
> With glass slippers ready to dance.

Prince sings:

> I don't know why I'm here this evening
> My dad thinks this dance is just great
> But I haven't seen any beauties
> And really it's getting quite late.
>
> Wait a minute
> Look who just came down the palace hall
> That's much better
> This may be fun after all.

Fairy Godmother's Magic
(fingerplay)

Fairy Godmother
Waves her wand
       (Wave imaginary wand back and forth.)
Over a pumpkin
Presto! It's gone
       (Clap hands.)
But look! there's a carriage
       (Point.)
with wheels
       (Roll hand over hand.)
and a door
But, wait—don't we need
something more?
       (Hands out, palms up as if asking.)
Six mice change to horses
       (Clap.)
We're ready to roll
       (Roll hand over hand.)
Whoa! Not so fast
       (Two hands up as if stopping action.)
Take a look at those clothes!
       (Shake head.)
With one last bit of magic
       (Wave imaginary wand again.)
She's the loveliest sight—
Now be off to the palace
       (Slide one palm over the other palm quickly.)
But be home by midnight!
       (Shake finger as a warning.)

Related Craft

Cinderella's Glad Rags

Using the paper doll and clothes on page 64, create a whole wardrobe for Cinderella to take to the palace. You may use bits of fabric and trims to glue on the clothes in addition to coloring them with markers.

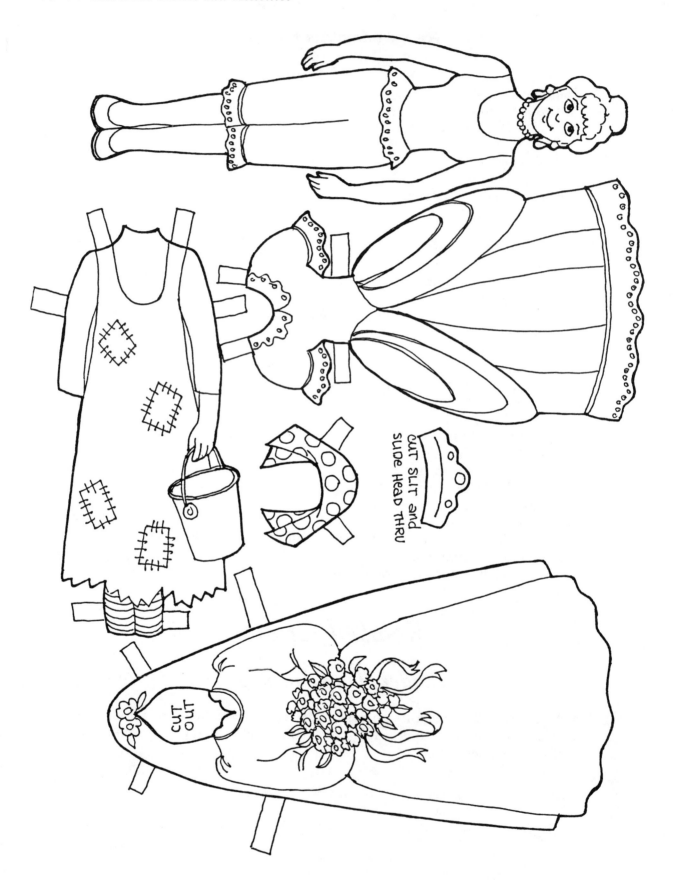

CUT SLIT and
SLIDE HEAD THRU

CUT OUT

Related Games

Time to Go Home
(a create-your-own game)

Divide into teams and let children make up games that show Cinderella hurrying home. They can brainstorm the types of games they know, and then adapt them. Some types of games are musical chairs, relay races, London Bridge, Simon Says.

For example, set up chairs for musical chairs. As you play dance music, everyone moves around the chairs. When the music stops, say "bong" twelve times. The children try to find a chair to sit down in before the clock chimes twelve. The child left standing joins you in making the clock chime. Take out a chair each round, and add another child to the chorus.

Footnotes

Hide Cinderella's shoe and let the group work together to find it! Write clues on shoe-shaped pieces of paper called "footnotes." One clue can lead to the next until the missing shoe is found. The children may want to divide into teams and hide the shoe again, creating their own footnotes for others to follow.

Related Skit

Watch Your Time!

Characters:

> Sidney
> Magical Person
> Royal Person
> assorted animals
> people at the ball

Plot: Sidney (either boy or girl) is left alone when everyone else goes to the ball. A Magic Person (male or female) appears and promises to help, but the magic is a little off base. Instead of changing white mice to horses, they turn into camels. Various other problems with the magic occur, but Sidney is a good sport. Finally Sidney is off to the ball. The party is fun and Sidney meets a Royal Person (prince or princess). Time flies and before long Sidney takes out a watch and notices it is time to go. Unfortunately the last magic is no better than the others: Sidney is transformed back into rags before the entire ball. No matter. This way the Royal Person doesn't waste time looking for Sidney. The Magic Person appears and tries again to make Sidney dressed up. The results are hilarious and there is a wedding on the spot.

Simple props and costumes will add interest to the presentation. Capes and long skirts will dress up the ball attendees. Use paper plates masks for the animals. By drawing a different face on each side of the plate, mice can "change into" camels by turning the mask around.

Related Cinderella Activities
(from other Irving and Currie books)

1. "Cinderella on a Tube," in *Glad Rags* (Libraries Unlimited, 1987), 128-129.

2. "Bumpkin in a Pumpkin," in *Full Speed Ahead* (Teacher Ideas Press, 1988), 181-183.

VI.
Little Red Riding Hood Stories and Activities

What Big Eyes You Have

The basic story line of this popular tale involves a little girl who is warned not to go into the forest or talk to strangers. When she disobeys, she and her grandmother are eaten by a wolf and must be saved by a passing woodcutter. The little girl vows never to disobey again. The series of similar exchanges between the girl and the wolf, now dressed in Grandma's nightcap, are often the most remembered elements.

"Oh, Grandma, what big eyes you have."
"All the better to see you with, my dear."
"Oh, Grandma, what big ears you have."
"All the better to hear you with, my dear."
"Oh, Grandma, what big teeth you have."
"All the better to eat you with, my dear."

The most familiar story comes from the Brothers Grimm and is called "Little Red Cap." Variants from other cultures include *Lon Po Po* from China, retold and illustrated by Ed Young, and winner of the 1989 Caldecott Medal. Another variant, "The Gunniwolf" begins with a little girl disobeying her mother by going into a jungle and meeting the Gunniwolf. There is no grandmother, and as no one is eaten (the little girl lulls the wolf to sleep with her "guten sweeten song"), this version is popular with early childhood educators.

Some recent versions of the tale have softened the violence found in earlier stories. Grandma and Red Riding Hood are not always eaten, nor is the wolf cut open and filled with rocks. On one hand, some educators feel these less violent versions are more appropriate for younger children. On the other hand, the dark nature of this story seems to have continuing appeal. Christopher Coady's very recent version uses thickly painted illustrations, heavy with shadows, to tell this cautionary tale. Trina Schart Hyman's version does not overlook the dangers, but she adds household details, wildflowers, and brighter colors. Beatrice de Regniers uses verse with such funny lines as this one: when Red Riding Hood emerges from the wolf's stomach she says, "Oh, it was smelly in there!"

The danger of strangers has always been an important story theme, and has taken on additional significance today as abductions increase. This is one tale not set in a contemporary time in picture-book form. It is terrifying enough in "once upon a time".

Our variant story tells the tale from Grandma's point of view. This will suggest to children that they may tell the same story from other points of view as well.

Booklist

Coady, Christopher. *Red Riding Hood*. Dutton, 1991.
    This recent retelling ends ominously with the wolf victorious. The endnote explains this as a cautionary tale, making this book better suited for older children to use in comparisons. Thickly painted illustrations heavy with shadows add to the terrifying mood.

Crawford, Elizabeth, translator. *Little Red Cap*. Illustrated by Lisbeth Zwerger. Morrow, 1983.
    Instead of a hood, this older girl wears a red silk cap in this softly illustrated edition. Taken from the Grimm version, Little Red Cap and her grandmother are rescued by the hunter, and Little Red Cap learns the importance of obeying her mother and staying on the path.

de Regniers, Beatrice Schenk. *Red Riding Hood*. Illustrated by Edward Gorey. Atheneum, 1972.
    Told in verse, this version features a wolf who gobbles up Grandma and Red Riding Hood. The hunter cuts open the wolf's belly to release the two and then fills the belly with stones. The verse is funny and the illustrations distinctive, with colors limited to pale beige and red.

Edens, Cooper. *Little Red Riding Hood*. Green Tiger Press, 1989.
    The preface gives a historical note and the text is traditional. Forty-six historical illustrations by such worthy artists as Arthur Rackham, Gustave Dore, and Jessie Wilcox Smith add to the fun of this edition.

Emberley, Michael. *Ruby*. Little, Brown, 1990.
    Ruby is a red-hooded, wise-cracking city mouse who is intercepted on her way to Granny's house by a velvety-voiced, impeccably dressed cat. Ruby is truly street-wise, and uses her wits to prevent what is usually inevitable. Hilarious text and illustrations work together to create a witty story.

Grimm, Jacob, and Wilhelm Grimm. *Little Red Riding Hood*. Illustrated by Ben Mahon. Troll, 1981.
    The wolf appears in "Jack the Ripper" clothing, and all characters are cartoon-like. The text is very short and appropriate for reading even to groups of young children.

Harper, Wilhemina. *The Gunniwolf*. Illustrated by William Wiesner. Dutton, 1970.
    In this variant, the little girl is warned not to go into the jungle because the gunniwolf might get her. As soon as the mother leaves, the girl sees white flowers growing on the edge of the jungle and she disobeys. As she wanders deeper into the jungle, she does meet the gunniwolf, who she repeatedly lulls to sleep with her "gutten sweeten song." This little girl escapes and promises never to disobey again.

Hyman, Trina Schart. *Little Red Riding Hood*. Holiday House, 1983.
  Lavish illustrations with intricate frames on each picture enhance this Caldecott Honor Book. In this version, the wolf is carried away for his pelt by the woodcutter after he is killed. There is a greater emphasis on the lesson Red Riding Hood learns: It is important to say "please" and "thank you."

Marshall, James. *Red Riding Hood*. Dial, 1987.
  Red Riding Hood and the wolf meet in the forest, and Red Riding Hood is charmed by his manners, even though she knows she should not talk to strangers. Meanwhile, Granny is an avid reader and is disturbed when the wolf arrives. He swallows her whole and waits in bed for Red Riding Hood, then eats her too. A passing hunter, alerted by the wolf's loud snoring, cuts the wolf open and saves them. The illustrations are colorful and amusing.

Neubacher, Gena. *Little Red Riding Hood*. Hayes, 1989.
  This story has pale pictures, and the story is altered to avoid any human-eating or wolf-chopping. Its short text is suitable for preschool groups that might be frightened by a harsher version.

Perrault, Charles. *Little Red Riding Hood*. Illustrated by Sarah Moon. Creative Education, 1983.
  This standard Perrault text, which ends with both Grandmamma and Red Riding Hood being eaten by the wolf, is made even more realistic by its use of stark, black-and-white photos. Not for the easily frightened, this powerful edition clearly shows the danger of talking to strangers.

Young, Ed. *Lon Po Po*. Philomel, 1989.
  Winner of the Caldecott Medal, this stunningly illustrated version of the Chinese tale features a good woman who leaves her three daughters at home when she goes to visit the granny. In the mother's absence, a wolf impersonates granny and gets into the house. The girls become wise to him, lure him up into a tree, and are triumphant in the end.

Traditional Story with Media Enhancement

  See the patterns for the stick puppets on page 71. Note that Grandma and the wolf each have a small piece of Velcro on their foreheads so the cap can be attached.

Red Riding Hood Retold

(Show Red Riding Hood puppet.) There was once a little girl who had a beautiful red cape and hood, so everyone called her Red Riding Hood. (Show mother puppet.) One day her mother sent her to her grandmother's house with a basket of goodies for her sick grandmother.

Before she left, her mother said, "Be sure to stay on the path and don't go into the woods. And don't talk to strangers." Red Riding Hood promised to do as she was told. But once she was in the woods, she forgot all her promises to her mother. (Put down mother puppet.)

(Show wolf puppet.) Then she met a wolf. The wolf asked, "Where are you going?"

Red Riding Hood said, "To Grandmother's house."

The wolf said, "I know a short cut. Go that way." (Put wolf puppet down.)

So Red Riding Hood followed the smaller path until it ran into a stream. Then Red Riding Hood realized this was not the best way. By the time she got back to the right path, a long time had passed. (Put Red Riding Hood puppet down.)

(Show wolf and Grandma.) The wolf had used that time to run ahead of Red Riding Hood to Grandmother's cottage. He put Grandma's nightcap on his head. (Move night cap to wolf head.) He stuffed Grandma in a closet (Put grandma down.) and crawled into her bed.

Soon there was a knock at the door.

"Come in," called the wolf in his sweetest voice.

(Show Red Riding Hood puppet.) When Red Riding Hood came into the room she thought grandma looked a little strange.

She said, "Grandma, what big eyes you have."

"All the better to see you with, my dear," said the wolf.

She came closer to the bed and said, "Grandma, what big ears you have."

"All the better to hear you with, my dear," said the wolf.

Then she came much closer and said, "Grandma, what big teeth you have."

The wolf jumped out of bed and shouted, "All the better to eat you with, my dear."

The wolf and Red Riding Hood ran around and around the cottage. The wolf almost caught Red Riding Hood when a passing woodcutter heard the noise and ran in. (Show Woodcutter.) The wolf took one look at the woodcutter with his big, sharp ax, and he ran out the door and was never seen again. (Put wolf down.)

Then Red Riding Hood and the woodcutter heard cries from the closet.

"It's Grandma!" said Red Riding Hood. (Show Grandma.) They let her out, and all sat down to enjoy the goodies Red Riding Hood had brought. (Put Grandma down.)

When it was time to go home the woodcutter walked part-way with Red Riding Hood. As they parted company he said, "Now stay on the path and don't talk to strangers." (Put woodcutter down.)

And this time, Red Riding Hood promised and did exactly as she was told.

Grandma's Side of the Story
(new story version)

Now, my granddaughter, Red, is just the sweetest thing, so friendly to everyone. Let me tell you about the day that friendliness almost got us both in a lot of trouble.

I had been feeling a mite poorly, even took to my bed. Little did I know how my strength would be tested!

I knew my daughter would be sending the child to visit me. That child is the prettiest thing with bright red hair. I made her a bright red cape and hood for her fifth birthday. It sure would cheer me up to see her. My daughter is a good baker and would probably fill a basket with some fine things to eat. I felt better just thinking about it. It seemed to take forever for her to get here. But she was not the first one to arrive!

Long about the time I expected Red, there was a knock on the door. I wasn't up to answering it so I called out, "Who is it?"

The voice answered, "It's me, your little granddaughter." Goodness, she must have had an awful cold for her voice to be that rough. But I told her to come in.

Lo and behold, it was a wolf a-knocking! He fairly chased me out of bed and around the room and knocked my cap clean off.

Now this next part will be a little gruesome, so some of you delicate types might wait outside. Well, here's what happened. The wolf just opened those jaws as wide as he could and - GULP - in one swallow I was in his stomach. Wheee! It really stunk in there. But I wasn't hurt and I could hear everything that went on.

So the wolf jumped into my bed and lay real still. And we heard another knock. It was Red.

Red came into the house. The wolf must have found my cap and put it on because she thought that it was me lying in the bed! But that Red, she is a sharp one. She began right away to see that something was wrong.

She told that wolf, "What big eyes you have."

But he was ready. "All the better to see you with," he said.

So Red said, "What big ears you have."

The old wolf snapped, "All the better to hear you with."

By now Red must have known something was up. She said, "What big teeth you have."

Then a hullabaloo started that I won't likely forget. That wolf yelled, "All the better to eat you with" and he jumped out of bed and swallowed her, too.

Now, I am always right glad to see my little Red, even if we were in a real tight spot. We hoped maybe a woodcutter would come along to save us, but we weren't that lucky. But that Red, she is a resourceful one. She slipped her hand into the basket and brought out her sewing shears. When the wolf was quiet and we could hear him snoring, she made a tidy little slit in the old coot's stomach and out we climbed. Free at last!

I got my sewing basket down, and after we filled that wolf with a few big stones we sewed him up. I showed Red how to do an overcast running stitch that time. I taught her everything she knows about sewing. Well, we shoved him out the door and that was the last we saw of him.

And what about that woodcutter? Well he never did show up. It is so hard to get good help these days. And as for us gals, we aren't as helpless as the storybooks say.

Literature Enrichment Activities

Writing Activity

Little Red Riding Hood Cards

There are greeting cards for every occasion and relationship! Let the children design cards that characters in the story would send to one another. For example. Grandmother might send a "Thank You" card to Red Riding Hood for the cakes. Red Riding Hood might send a get-well card to Grandmother.

Speaking Activities

Red Riding Hood's Forest Song
(Tune: "When Johnny Comes Marching Home")

I'm going to granny's house today
Beware! Beware!
I'm going to granny's house today
Beware! Beware!
The woods are dark and I'm all alone
I'm going to grandmother's on my own
I'll just go my way now
Through the dark woods alone.

I'm here at Granny's house at last
Knock knock. Knock knock.
Who's that in Grandma's house who calls
Come in, come in?
There are great big eyes and some great big ears
And great big teeth I deeply fear
And I don't think Grandma
Looks very good today.

Big Eyes, Big Ears, Big Teeth
(fingerplay)

The wolf puts on Granny's cap
> (Pat head.)
And crawls in Granny's bed
> (Rest head on hands.)
He puts on Granny's glasses
> (Circle eyes with fingers.)
And calls for Little Red
> (Cup hands around mouth.)
She says his eyes are big
> (Circle eyes with fingers.)
She says his ears are long
> (Touch top of head and raise hands as if feeling long ears.)
She says his teeth are very sharp
> (Point to teeth.)
His jaws look very strong
> (Clamp teeth together.)
But when he starts to chase her
> (Run in place.)
Little Red runs away
> (Run faster.)
She calls for a woodcutter
> (Cup hands around mouth.)
He comes to save the day
> (Make arm muscle.)

Related Craft

Red Riding Hood's Basket

Using the pattern on page 75, make a basket from brightly colored construction paper. Attach a handle made from brightly colored yarn or another strip of paper. Fill the basket with flowers or little treats to take to your grandmother.

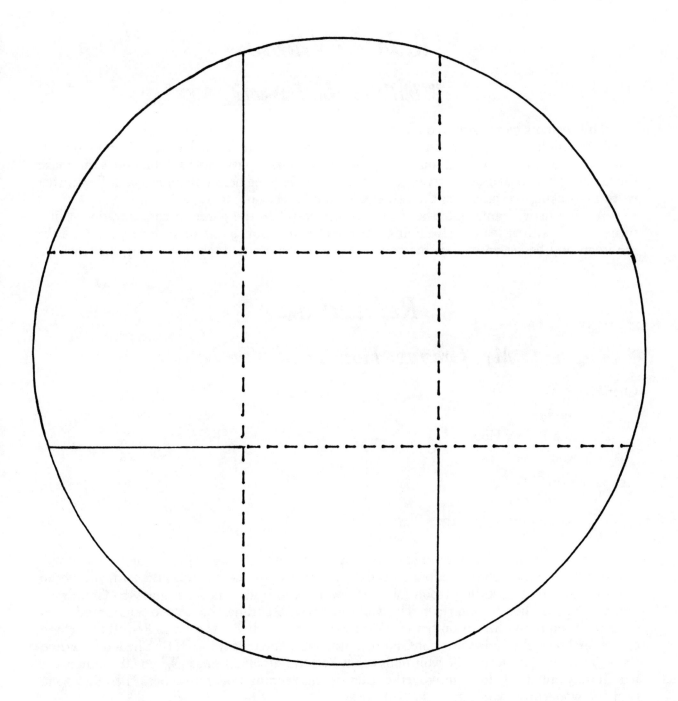

Related Game

What's in the Basket?

This memory game is played like the traditional "I Unpacked My Grandmother's Trunk," in which children compile a list of objects they would put in Red Riding Hood's basket. Younger children can just add something they would take to grandma's. Older ones can make the list in alphabetical order or try to remember what everyone before them has said. For further writing/speaking activities, list the contents of the basket on paper.

An alternative game tests the children's memory like the game of concentration. Fill a picnic basket with at least twelve items. Let the children look at the items for a minute. Take the items and basket away and challenge the children to write down everything they saw.

Related Skit

My, Granny, How Tired You Look!

Characters:

> mother
> Red Riding Hood
> wolf
> Grandma
> woodcutter
> forest animals and trees

Plot: Mother warns Red Riding Hood to be careful in the woods when going to Grandma's house. While in the woods, the forest animals and trees warn her to stay on the path and not to talk to strangers. Red Riding Hood meets the wolf, who finds out she is going to Grandma's house. He points her to a short-cut. The wolf runs on to Grandma's house and puts Grandma in a closet. Then the wolf puts on her night cap and gets into bed. As soon as Red Riding Hood enters the house she knows it is not Granny in the bed. She tells the wolf that he looks so tired she will sing him to sleep. The wolf nods off as Red Riding Hood sings. When all is quiet, she lets Granny out of the closet and together they tie the sleeping wolf with ropes. Then they go to find the woodcutter who carries the wolf away.

Note: In this skit, the children know the basic storyline and they create their own lines of dialogue as they think the characters might say them.

Simple props and costumes will add interest to the presentation. Make a wolf mask from the pattern on page 77. Red Riding Hood can wear something red, such as a red scarf or a red

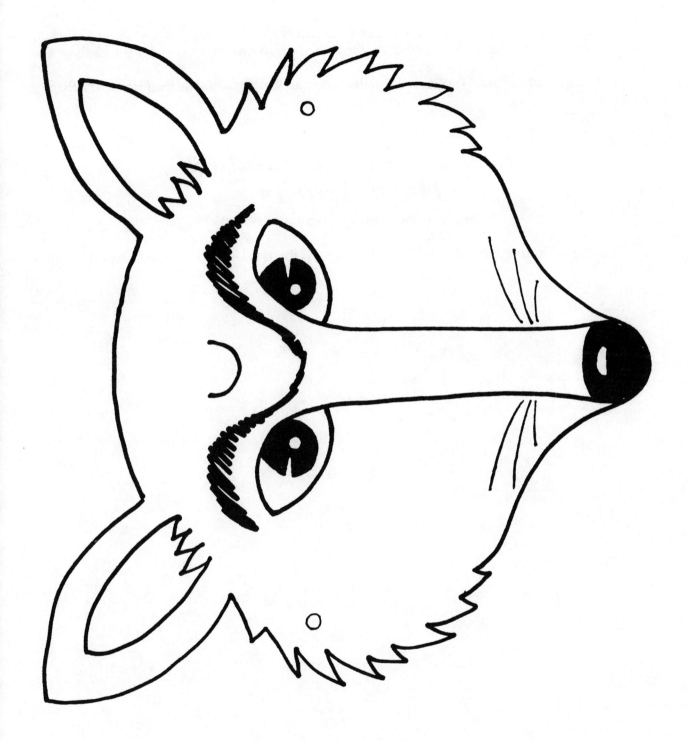

T-shirt. Grandma wears a simple bonnet. Cut a 12-inch circle of material. Sew a running stitch three inches from the outer edge, and draw the thread up to make a bonnet for the head of a child.

Put ears on a headband for forest animals. Trees can wear headbands with leaves attached to them.

Related Little Red Riding Hood Activity
(from another Irving and Currie book)

1. "Little Red Riding Hood Retold," in *Glad Rags* (Libraries Unlimited, 1987), 132-134.

VII.
Jack and the Beanstalk Stories and Activities

Fee Fie Foe Fum

The story of a small man slaying a giant dates to ancient times. The Biblical David slaying Goliath, or the Greek myth of Odysseus wounding the Cyclops, appeals to our own desire to "slay" those bigger and more powerful. In a classed society, peasants readily identified with the underdog much in the same way that children feel their world is peopled with giants.

Jack and the Beanstalk originally came from England, but it has variants in the Appalachian region of the United States where the title becomes "Jack and the Bean Tree." In all the versions, Jack trades the cow for magic beans which grow into a beanstalk up to a land of giants. Here Jack usually meets the giant's wife, who hides him when the giant comes home. While the giant sleeps, Jack first steals a bag of gold. On later visits he takes a hen who lays golden eggs, and a singing harp. When the giant chases Jack as he gets away with the harp, Jack chops down the beanstalk and the giant falls to his death. Jack and his mother have enough treasures to last the rest of their days. These objects vary in some stories, and occasionally Jack is merely taking back what the giant stole from his father.

The picture books include more traditional versions such as Lorinda Bryan Cauley's, or Paul Galdone's based on the 1807 poem about Mother Twaddle and her son Jack, and modern retellings by Steven Kellogg and Tim Paulsen. Kellogg's story is full of running, climbing, chopping, and falling so the illustrations are especially lively. Tim Paulsen's two-story format is unique because it reminds us that stories can be told from different perspectives.

Traditionally, the hero of this tale is male. In our version, Jill uses her wits to win the giant's heart. You might want to look for some other traditional stories where females play an active role, such as the English folktale of Mollie Whuppie. Students might enjoy writing their own updated versions of folk tales in which females play active roles. Suzanne Barcher's collection, *Wise Women: Folk and Fairy Tales from around the World* (Libraries Unlimited, 1990), is an excellent source of stories in which females are "heroic for their ingenuity and resourcefulness."

Jack continues to be a favorite hero because he is the underdog. Everyday people like to fantasize they are capable of winning and finding undiscovered worlds and treasures, underwater, out in space, or up a beanstalk.

Booklist

Briggs, Raymond. *Jim and the Beanstalk*. Coward McCann, 1970.

When Jim meets the giant, the big guy is no longer able to eat boys or even read the fine print in his poetry books. Jim fits him with glasses and false teeth (much to the amazement of the people back on earth who make them!). The final touch is a red-haired wig for the giant. All spruced up again, the giant feels so young he advises Jim to go and chop down the beanstalk or the giant might cause big trouble.

Cauley, Lorinda Bryan. *Jack and the Beanstalk*. Putnam's, 1983.

This is a very traditional telling of the Jack who climbs the beanstalk to the land of giants. Oil-painted illustrations add to the "once upon a time" mood of the story.

de Regniers, Beatrice Schenk. *Jack and the Beanstalk*. Illustrated by Ann Wilsdorf. Macmillan, 1990.

Told in free verse and using a vocabulary that's easy enough for beginning readers, this version of the story shows Jack stealing from the giant only the things the giant took from Jack's own father years before. The text and pictures are cleverly interwoven, and give a sense of being in the bean vines.

Francois, Andre. *Jack and the Beanstalk*. Creative Education, 1983.

Modern illustrations done in chalk, crayon, and watercolors shows the giant's wife as a cyclops, and the giant as an ogre. The text is a faithful retelling, with Jack not only getting rich, but marrying the princess as well.

Galdone, Paul. *Jack and the Beanstalk*. Clarion, 1974.

The text is the verse version of the traditional story originally published as *Mother Twaddle*, and the marvelous achievements of her son, Jack, in 1807. Galdone adds lively illustrations that make the action come right off the page.

Haley, Gail. *Jack and the Bean Tree*. Crown, 1986.

This mountain-language retelling of Jack's adventures with the giant Ephidophilus includes a magic tablecloth, a hen who lays golden eggs, and a golden harp. When Jack steals these, the giant accuses his neighbors and starts fights, but the wife Matilda, has a soft spot for Jack and keeps letting him in. Even after the beanstalk is felled and the giant is dead, Jack wonders how Matilda is getting along in "skyland." The pictures are done on woodboards and modeled from a set of puppets made to tell the story in a multimedia presentation.

Kellogg, Steven. *Jack and the Beanstalk*. Morrow, 1991.

Kellogg's typically hilarious illustrations provide an exciting interpretation of the traditional story of magic beans. The giant and his wife are particularly unique. Don't miss the details on every page, including a drawing of Pinkerton in the last picture.

Paulsen, Tim. *Jack and the Beanstalk* and *The Beanstalk Incident*. Carol, 1992.

In the first story, the reader hears the traditional tale of Jack and the Beanstalk. Then turn the book upside down to read the story as told by the giant's goose that lays golden eggs. In the latter tale, the giant is the victim of a break-in.

Pearson, Susan. *Jack and the Beanstalk*. Illustrated by James Warhola. Simon & Schuster, 1989.
    Faithful retelling of Jack's adventures in the clouds. Bright illustrations make the giant big but not frightening. The perspective of some drawings is from the top of the beanstalk looking down. Spectacular!

Traditional Story with Media Enhancement

In most of the tube stories we have found, the tube is held horizontally with the figures raised and lowered. This story uses the tube as a beanstalk so, of course, it is held vertically when Jack climbs up the beanstalk. You will want to use a long tube, the kind wrapping paper comes on, for a tall beanstalk effect. Cover the tube with green construction paper.

Use the patterns on pages 84 and 85 to make figures for the story. Cut out the figures and attach each to a strip of lightweight posterboard or cardboard with brad fasteners. The figures can then be turned to change positions as the cardboard tube is moved from a horizontal to a vertical position. Staple the ends of the strip to form a ring that will slip over the cardboard tube. Attach a small piece of Velcro to the gold, the hen, and the harp, so they can be removed from the giant's table and placed in Jack's hand later in the story. Now you are ready to tell the story with all the figures hanging below the tube. The tube is held horizontally to begin the story.

Jack and the Beanstalk Retold

Once upon a time there was a poor woman who lived with her son, Jack (raise woman and Jack so they can be seen above the tube). The old woman sent Jack to town to sell their only cow so they would have money enough to eat. (Lower woman.)

Well, Jack didn't exactly sell the cow. He traded the cow for three magic beans. (Raise picture of beans.) Jack took the beans home to show his mother. (Raise woman.) But Jack's mother was furious that Jack had traded their cow for three lousy beans. Jack's mother was so mad she threw those beans out the window and sent Jack to bed. (Lower all three figures.)

But, in the night, those beans grew and grew and grew. When Jack woke up the next morning, what do you think he saw outside his window? That's right! Jack saw a big beanstalk growing outside. (Now turn the tube vertically as the beanstalk grows.) Jack crawled out of the window and climbed up that beanstalk. (Raise Jack figure and turn it around, as if Jack is climbing the beanstalk, and move figure up the tube.)

Jack climbed and he climbed and he climbed (move figure up tube) until he got to the top. There he saw an enormous castle with a big woman outside. (Raise giant's wife.)

"Good morning, my name's Jack," said Jack. "Won't you give me some breakfast?"

"Breakfast?" said the woman, "You'd better get on out of here. My husband's a big, mean giant, and he'll likely eat YOU for his breakfast."

"Aw, please," said Jack.

"Well, all right, but you'd better be fast about it," said the giant's wife.

Now, very soon after Jack had gone inside he heard a big THUMP THUMP THUMP in the front hall.

"That's him, the giant. Quick, hide in the pantry," said the giant's wife. (Lower Jack. Raise giant.)

"Fee Fie Foe Fum,
I smell trouble that's about to come.
If he's large or if he's small
I'll gobble him up, toes and all," thundered the giant.

"You only smell ox stew. Here, eat your dinner, dear," said the giant's wife.

So the giant ate, and then he put his gold on the table and counted it. (Raise table with gold on it.) But the giant had eaten so much stew that he quickly fell asleep. (Lower giant.)

Jack jumped out of the pantry (raise Jack), grabbed the gold (remove gold, and stick on Jack's hand), and slid down the beanstalk. (Move Jack down the beanstalk.)

Jack gave his mother the gold (raise Mother), and with the money they lived happily for many days. One day when most of the money was gone, Jack decided to go back up the beanstalk. (Take the gold from Jack's hand and put it in your lap. Move Jack figure up the beanstalk.)

Jack climbed and he climbed and he climbed (move figure up tube) until he got to the top. There he saw an enormous castle again with the giant's wife outside. (Raise giant's wife.)

He didn't ask the giant's wife for anything this time. He just tiptoed into the house and hid in the corner of the front hall. (Lower Jack.)

Now, very soon after Jack had gone inside, he heard a big THUMP THUMP THUMP in the front hall. (Raise giant.)

"Fee Fie Foe Fum,
I smell trouble that's about to come.
If he's large or if he's small
I'll gobble him up, toes and all," thundered the giant.

"I haven't seen anyone. You only smell ox stew. Here, eat your dinner, dear," said the giant's wife.

So the giant ate and then he put his goose on the table. (Raise table with goose on it.) The goose was magic because it laid golden eggs. The giant watched the goose lay three eggs, and then he fell asleep. (Lower giant.)

Jack sneaked out of the corner (raise Jack), grabbed the hen (remove hen, and stick on Jack's hand), and slid down the beanstalk. (Move Jack down the beanstalk.)

Jack gave the hen to his mother (raise mother) and again they lived happily for many days. (Take hen from Jack's hand and put in your lap.) Finally, one day Jack got restless and went back up the beanstalk. (Lower mother and move Jack up beanstalk.)

Jack climbed and he climbed and he climbed (move figure up tube) until he got to the top. There he saw an enormous castle again, with the giant's wife outside. (Raise giant's wife.)

He didn't ask the giant's wife for anything this time. He just tiptoed into the house and hid behind the curtains. (Lower Jack.)

Now, very soon after Jack had gone inside, he heard a big THUMP THUMP THUMP in the front hall. (Raise giant.)

"Fee Fie Foe Fum,
I smell trouble that's about to come.
If he's large or if he's small
I'll gobble him up, toes and all," thundered the giant.

"I haven't seen anyone. You only smell ox stew. Here, eat your dinner, dear," said the giant's wife.

So the giant ate and ate, and then he put his harp that sang all by itself on the table. (Raise harp.) The harp sang so sweetly that the giant fell asleep.

Jack sneaked out from behind the curtains (raise Jack), grabbed the harp (remove harp, and stick it on Jack's hand), and slid down the beanstalk. (Start to slide Jack down.)

But the harp started to call to the giant. The giant woke up and chased Jack. (Raise giant and start sliding him down the beanstalk.)

Jack ran faster and faster. The giant was coming faster and faster. (Slide Jack and giant down beanstalk.) Jack went faster and faster, and as soon as he was home he got his ax and chopped down that beanstalk. (Dramatically lower beanstalk onto your lap.) And that was the end of the giant.

So Jack and his mother lived out the rest of their days happily ever after.

STRIPS are APPROX. 1" x 8"

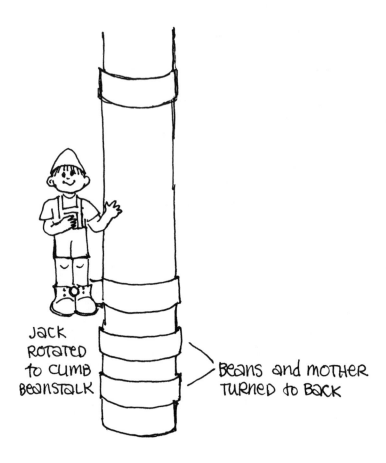

JACK
ROTATED
to CLIMB
BEANSTALK

Beans and MOTHER
TURNED to BACK

Jill and the Beanstalk
(new story version)

Jill loved garage sales. Every weekend she went this way and that way, and even out of the way to find the best bargains. She found treasures in everyone else's trash.

One day, she went to a sale down a country lane and into a forest where she found a most unusual cottage. Even more unusual, there was only one item left for sale. It was a cooking pot, sooty and old. But it was the only thing on sale, so Jill bought it.

When she got the cooking pot home she cleaned it up and looked inside. There was a handful of beans. "Hmm," she wondered. "What if these were magic beans like that boy, Jack, found?" And just to be on the safe side, she did not eat the beans but tossed them out the window into the garden.

Now, Jill did not really believe the Jack story until the next morning. There outside her window was a beanstalk, growing every minute toward the sky. Jill climbed on a leaf and rode all the way to the top.

There she saw the huge castle. "This all seems very familiar to me," she said. "I wonder if there is a giant in there?" The only way to find out was to go and ask. So that's what she did.

Now, you may think that the giant died at the end of that story, but the truth is that he made an amazing recovery. In the years since Jack had visited him the giant had grown older. The giant simply did not feel like chasing anybody. He preferred to spend his days working the Giant Crossword Puzzles in the "Daily News." And he loved riddles.

So when Jill came knocking at the giant's door, he was glad to have company. Instead of roaring, the giant called out,
Fee, fie, foe, fiddle!
Can you guess this tricky riddle?

Jill was a clever lass and loved games, so she said,
Riddle me, riddle me, riddle me, ree
I'll guess any riddle you give to me.
I've come a long way. Is it worth my time?
What will you give me if I guess your rhyme?

The giant was delighted to match wits with Jill, so he said,
Fee, fie, foe, fiddle!
Your prize is hidden in the riddle.

And the giant's first riddle was,
This has teeth but cannot chew
But it can open doors for you.

Jill thought before she answered. Do any of you think you can answer the riddle? (Take suggestions.) Finally Jill knew the answer: "A key!"

"Correct," said the giant. "Here is the key to my tower. It's my favorite place and there is a wonderful treasure inside."

So Jill and the giant went to the tower. When they got there, they used her key to open the door. But before they went in the giant said,
>Fee, fie, foe, fiddle!
>Can you guess this tricky riddle?

Jill said,
>Riddle me, riddle me, riddle me, ree
>I'll guess any riddle you give to me.
>I've come a long way. Is it worth my time?
>What will you give me if I guess your rhyme?

The giant answered,
>Fee, fie, foe, fiddle!
>Your prize is hidden in the riddle.

And the giant's second riddle was,
>This has leaves but is not a tree
>It is bound but it can set you free.

So Jill thought again. Leaves. Bound. Can you guess? (Take suggestions.) Jill suddenly said, "A book! It's a book!"

The tower was full of books. Jill ran from one room to the other. She loved books. "This is wonderful!" she said. "Better than any treasure I ever uncovered in a garage sale."

The giant was so happy to see someone who loved books as much as he did that he made a decision right then and there. Jill could stay with him forever. So he told her,
>Fee, fie, foe, fiddle!
>Can you guess this tricky riddle?

Jill said,
>Riddle me, riddle me, riddle me, ree
>I'll guess any riddle you give to me.
>I've come a long way. Is it worth my time?
>What will you give me if I guess your rhyme?

The giant answered,
>Fee, fie, foe, fiddle!
>Your prize is hidden in the riddle

And the giant's third riddle was,
>Golden circle, sound of a bell
>My secret heart you know so well.

Jill thought and thought and thought. Can you guess what the riddle was? (Take suggestions.) Jill told the giant,
>The sound of a bell must be a ring
>And a golden circle is the same thing!

"Right!" said the giant. "You win the ring and my heart. We can spend our lives reading here together."

So Jill and the giant lived—as they say in storybooks—happily ever after.

Literature Enrichment Activities

Writing Activities

Jack's Place

Because the giant's castle is unoccupied, Jack looks to make this property into a real estate opportunity. The children can decide what the giant's castle and grounds might become, and then develop an advertising campaign to promote this new attraction. The children can create newspaper ads, TV or radio spots, posters or flyers.

For example, if Jack decides to make the giant's bathtub into an olympic pool, his TV spot could say: "Hey, kids! You'll make a big splash when you invite the whole school to a swimming party at Jack's Place. Jack's—The place for big fun!"

Song of the Golden Harp

Children will enjoy composing their own songs for the golden harp. You could suggest a tune such as "Twinkle, Twinkle Little Star" or "My Bonnie Lies Over the Ocean," then divide children into small groups to write the songs. After all the groups have completed their songs, have everyone share them. Comparing and contrasting songs on the same topic will show children the many different ways a subject can be approached.

Speaking Activities

Almost Jack Splat!
(action rhyme)

Jack climbed the giant, starting at his toes
    (Wiggle fingers by foot.)
Up past his knee so quietly he goes
    (Wiggle fingers by knee.)
Climbing very carefully right across his lap
    (Wiggle fingers across lap.)
But when he climbs the giant's arm, the giant answers with a SLAP!
    (Slap arm loudly.)

Luckily for Jack he's in another place
    (Point to underside of arm.)
Up the giant's shoulder Jack starts to climb his face,
    (Wiggle fingers up face.)
Then teeth and nose and eyebrows, Jack will never stop
    (Touch parts mentioned.)
He won't be contented until he sees the top!
    (Stand up, arms outstretched.)

Fee Fie Foe Fum
(chant)

Pause after every two lines to allow the children to repeat them. Set the rhythm by slapping hands on legs.

Heard about Jack
And the magic beans?
Traded for the cow,
Or so it seems.
Up with the stalk,
And Jack did, too.
Knocked on the door
And called "Yoo hoo!"
The giant called back
"Fee, fie, foe, fum
Seems like my dinner's
Finally come."
But Jack he hid
Till the giant snored,
Then grabbed the goose
And made for the door.
With the giant behind
Jack slid to the ground,
Chopped that stalk
Till the giant fell down.

Climbing the Beanstalk
(Tune: "Down by the Station")

Climbing up the beanstalk
To the very top
Met an angry giant there
Who loudly hollered "stop!"
Jack grabbed the golden goose
And never did look back
Finally killed the giant when
He gave the stalk a whack.

The Short End of the Stalk
(Tune: "Up on the House Top")

Add extra fun to singing this song by adding actions that children suggest to you. They will all, no doubt, suggest chopping actions for the line "Chop, chop, chop." Do this with great gusto in the spirit of the story.

Up on the beanstalk
Jack looks back,
Golden harp stuck
In his pack.
Here comes the giant
Nine feet tall,
Jack feels very
Very small.
Fee, Fie, Foe
Fum Fum Fum
Look out Jack
Now here I come!
Jack whacks the beanstalk
Chop, chop, chop!
That's where the story
Has to stop!

Related Craft

Giant Step

The giant, Ephidophilus, in Gail Haley's *Jack and the Bean Tree*, wears sandals that Jack ties together. Give the children photocopies of the giant foot and sandal from page 91. They can color the giant foot, then take a piece of yarn to insert in the holes to make the laces for the sandal. With these sandals any giant will be able to take big giant steps.

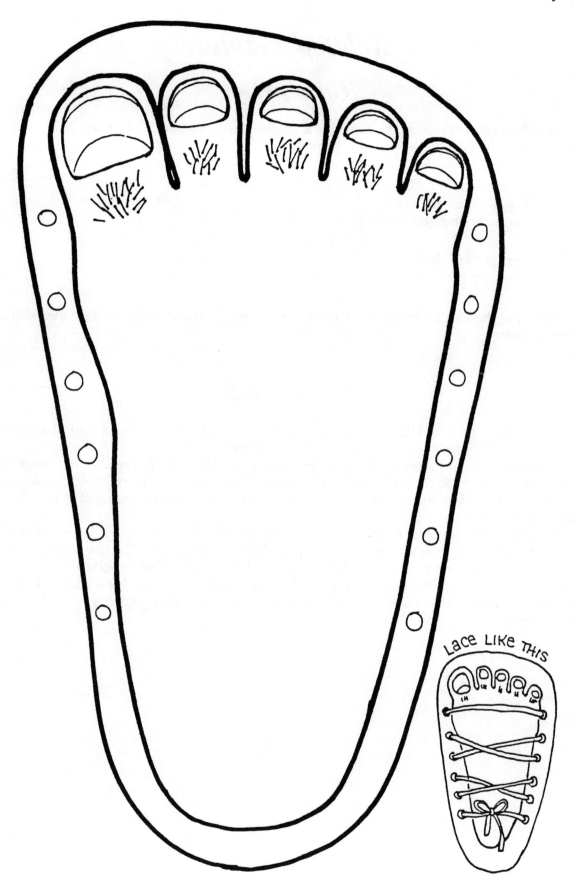

Lace Like This

Related Games

Giant's Play

Use the giant's rhyme as the basis for a rhyming action game. You make up a two-line verse and the children do the action suggested.

For example:

> Fee, fie, foe, fip
> Show me how you can skip

> Fee, fie, foe, fun
> Show me how you can run

Once the children understand the format, encourage them to make up their own rhymes to other actions.

After the Fall

Tell children that after the beanstalk fell, it made a terrible mess in Jack's yard. But instead of cleaning it up or moving, Jack made it into an obstacle course.

Children learn to follow numbers in sequence with this activity. Cut 20 to 25 large leaf shapes out of green paper, and number them. Tape the leaves on chairs, tables, desks, and shelves. Children then follow the leaves in numerical order and end up going up, down, around, and under.

Vary the games for older children by writing clues on each leaf. Each clue leads children to discover the next leaf. The first leaf might read, "The beanstalk fell. The first leaf landed in your hand. The next one went to a land where the wild things are." The second clue then might be on a library shelf with the book *Where the Wild Things Are*. The last clue leads children to a place where a bag of jelly beans is buried. An alternative prize might be a bag of seeds for the class to plant.

Related Skit

Who's That Climbing Up My Beanstalk?

Characters:

> Giant
> Jack or Jackie
> Mother
> cow
> man selling beans
> bag of gold
> golden goose
> talking harp

Plot: The giant recounts the story of Jack's visits up the beanstalk. Jack's mother sends her son to market with the cow that he trades to a man for some magic beans. Jack's mother throws the beans out the window. These grow into a huge beanstalk that Jack climbs. The giant shouts down to Jack, "Who's climbing my beanstalk?" Jack visits the giant three times, each time stealing one of the treasures: a bag of gold, a golden goose, a harp. The giant chases Jack after the lad steals the harp. Jack quickly climbs down and chops down the beanstalk. The giant narrowly escapes falling from the beanstalk by jumping to the ground. He lands so hard that where he landed he made a big hole and that hole turned into Lake (use the name of a lake near your town).

Note: In this skit, the children know the basic storyline and then create their own lines of dialogue as they think the characters might say them.

Props: Simple props and costumes will add interest to the presentations. Cut out shapes of cardboard for the bag of gold, goose, and harp. A little gold glitter on these will add to the fun. A cow can be made by covering two children with a sheet or blanket. To make the giant, cover an empty cereal box with paper and draw on the giant's features for his head. Attach this head to a broomstick and hold high so the giant will be taller than the others.

VIII.
Stone Soup
Stories
and Activities

More Than Enough

The cooking-pot motif appears in two different story lines. In one, the cooking pot produces an abundance of a particular food (rice, pasta, porridge) when the proper magic is used. The prototype for this story is "Sweet Porridge," as told by the Brothers Grimm. The magic may be words that are misunderstood or not complete when the wrong person takes charge, so the pot goes berserk. Order is restored when the rightful owner of the pot uses the magic as it was intended. In the other story line, soup or stew is produced from seemingly nothing at all. The soup begins with a stone or nail, and the promise of enough to feed everyone if others will contribute what they have. The prototype for this story is *Stone Soup* as retold by Marcia Brown.

The stone soup story comes from France, but it crosses cultures to appear as nail broth in Sweden or boiled ax or hatchet gruel in Russia. The sweet porridge story comes from Germany, but it becomes *The Funny Little Woman* (retold by Arlene Mosel) cooking rice dumplings in Japan, and *Strega Nona* (retold by Tomie dePaola) cooking pasta in Italy.

These stories invite children to act them out, or write their own versions as they might appear in their own neighborhoods or in other cultures. Any unlikely object might start a soup, as shown in our own "Shoe Stew" (see pp. 99-100). Imaginative thinking and problem-solving skills can be practiced as children tell how magic pots can be stopped, or what can be done with a town buried in spaghetti.

Booklist

Brenner, Barbara. *Group Soup*. Illustrated by Lynn Munsinger. Viking, 1992.

This add-an-ingredient story has no magic "starter" (such as a stone or nail). There is one uncooperative grumpy rabbit who will not contribute to the soup or believe it will be any good until she tries it. Then she adds parsley and the soup is delicious. Includes a song about sharing.

Brown, Marcia. *Stone Soup*. Prentice-Hall, 1974.

This French folktale has become a modern classic about three soldiers who teach a village how to make soup out of stones. Even very young children will understand the humorous trickery.

dePaola, Tomie. *Strega Nona*. Prentice-Hall, 1975.

Strega Nona (Grandma Witch) warns Big Anthony, her helper, never to touch her magic pasta pot. But the moment she goes to visit a friend, he tries it out—much to the alarm of this small Italian town that becomes buried in pasta.

Ginsburg, Mirra. *The Magic Stove*. Illustrated by Linda Heller. Coward-McCann, 1983.

An old man, his wife, and a rooster, enjoy pies made by a magic stove until the king steals it from them. The rooster outsmarts the king, so the stove is returned and makes pies for the couple again.

Greene, Ellin, compiler. "The Old Woman Who Lost her Dumpling," from *Clever Cooks*. Illustrated by Trina Schart Hyman. Lothrop, Lee & Shepard, 1973.

In this Japanese tale, a funny old woman chases her rice dumpling beneath the earth where she meets an oni (an ogre) who gives her a magic rice paddle. Eventually she takes the paddle back to her home, where she makes rice dumplings to feed neighbors and friends.

Hirsch, Marilyn. *Potato Pancakes All Around*. Bonim, 1978.

A wandering peddler teaches a village family how to make potato pancakes from only a crust of bread so they can have a happy Hanukkah. A recipe for potato pancakes is included.

Hong, Lily Toy. *Two of Everything*. Albert Whitman, 1993.

The Haktaks have a wonderful new pot: when they throw in a hairpin, two come out. When they throw in a coin, two come out. But one day Mr. Haktak falls into the pot. When there are suddenly two Mr. Haktaks, the trouble begins.

McGovern, Ann. *Stone Soup*. Illustrated by Winslow Pinney Pels. Scholastic, 1986.

A hungry young man shows a little old lady how to make soup out of a stone. The old woman's ingredients from her garden help to make the soup fit for a king.

Mosel, Arlene. *The Funny Little Woman*. Illustrated by Blair Lent. Dutton, 1972.

The funny little woman follows a rolling dumpling to the underworld, where she stays to make rice dumplings for the wicked Oni. She escapes with a magic paddle that will make all the rice dumplings she wants, and she becomes the richest woman in Japan.

Stewig, John Warren. *Stone Soup*. Illustrated by Margot Tomes. Holiday House, 1991.

Grethel and her mother have a hard life, so Grethel sets out to make her own way. When she is unable to get a meal in a nearby village she comes up with a plan. She shows the villagers how to make soup from a stone and knows she will always have something to eat.

Zemach, Harve. *Nail Soup*. Illustrated by Margot Zemach. Follett, 1964.

A tramp cannot beg any food from the old woman until he teaches her to make soup from a nail. The trick, of course, is to add something good—meat, potatoes, milk, and so on—until the nail soup is fit for a king.

Traditional Story
with Media Enhancement

This story uses actual objects, or soft sculpture versions of them, as children participate in the telling. Assemble the following objects for the story: a cooking pot, three stones, four carrots, six potatoes, a piece of beef, milk, barley, a loaf of bread, and a jug of cider. Distribute the items to children and instruct them to place them in the pot at the appropriate time.

Stone Soup

One day, three travelers wandered down the road. They were tired and hungry and were glad to see a village in the near distance.

"Perhaps someone will give us a place to sleep," said John, the first traveler.

"And something to eat," said David, the second traveler.

"I'm hopeful," said William, the third traveler.

As the travelers approached the village, all the people looked out of the houses and were afraid the travelers would take all their good food. So the people hid everything they had.

The travelers stopped first at the house of Maria and Tony.

"Could you spare something to eat?" asked John.

"We have nothing to share," said Maria.

The travelers then went to the house of Nathaniel and Helen.

"Could you spare something to eat?" asked David.

"We have nothing to share," said Nathaniel.

The travelers then went to the house of Jacob and Hannah.

"Could you spare something to eat?" asked David.

"We have nothing to share," said Hannah.

And so it was, house after house. Nobody had anything to share.

Finally, the three travelers called all the townspeople together in the town square.

"Good people," they said, "we know that times have been hard for you. We would now like to share our secret recipe with you."

"Secret recipe?" questioned Hannah.

"Yes," said John. "Our secret recipe for stone soup."

"We will be most happy to share it with you," said David.

"If you will bring us a pot full of water," said William, "and three round stones."

"Three stones?" asked Nathaniel.

"Three stones," said William.

So Nathaniel and Tony and Jacob brought a big pot full of water, and into the pot they put the three stones.

The travelers stirred and stirred the water and the stones.

"This is good," said John.

"But it would be better," said David.

"If only we had some carrots," said William.

Maria hurried home, got four fat carrots, brought them back and put them in the pot.

The travelers stirred and stirred the water and the stones.

"This is good," said John.

"But it would be better," said David.

"If only we had some potatoes," said William.

Helen hurried home, got six potatoes, brought them back and put them in the pot.

The travelers stirred and stirred the water and the stones.

"This is good," said John.

"But it would be better," said David.

"If only we had some beef," said William.

Hannah hurried home, got a piece of beef, and brought it back to put in the pot.

The travelers stirred and stirred the water and the stones.

"This is good," said John.

"But it would be better," said David.

"If only we had some milk and barley," said William.

Tony hurried home, got milk and barley, brought them back to put in the pot.

The travelers stirred and stirred the water and the stones.

"This is good," said John.

"But it would be fit for a king," said David.

"If only we had bread and cider," said William.

So Nathaniel and Jacob hurried home. Nathaniel brought a loaf of bread and Jacob brought a jug of cider.

When the men returned, everyone was setting up tables for the feast. John and David and William served big bowls of their secret recipe of stone soup. Everyone agreed it was fit for a king.

After the feast, the three travelers slept in the homes of Tony and Maria, Nathaniel and Helen, and Jacob and Hannah. The next morning John and David and William set off on a new journey.

"Now you will never be hungry," said John.

"You can always make stone soup," said David.

"Just remember the secret recipe," said William.

And everyone always did.

Shoe Stew

(new story version)

Once, a traveler arrived in a small seaside village with nothing but the shirt on his back and the shoes on his feet. He longed to take the weight off his feet and have something to eat. But the people in the town told him the fishing had been very bad that day and there was nothing in the town to eat at all.

Instead of complaining the traveler said, "Let me help you, then. I'll show you how to make a stew so you will never be hungry again. We'll make stew from my shoe!"

"Stew from a shoe?" they said.

The traveler promised, "Bring me a pot and build a fire, and tonight we'll eat the finest shoe stew in all the seven seas!"

So they brought him a pot of water and built a fire. The traveler took off his left shoe and dropped it into the pot. He stirred and stirred and stirred. Then he sniffed the stew and said,

> Stir and slosh, through and through
> This is how we make shoe stew

He stirred and stirred and sniffed the stew. Then the traveler said, "I don't want to muscle in, but some mussels would make this shoe stew the finest in all the seven seas!"

And, wonder of wonders, one of the people in the seaside village had some mussels to put in the pot. The traveler stirred and stirred and stirred. Then he sniffed the stew and said,

> Stir and slosh, through and through
> This is how we make shoe stew

He stirred and stirred and sniffed the stew. Then the traveler said, "I don't want to be a crab, but some crab legs would make this shoe stew the finest in all the seven seas!"

And wonder of wonders, one of the villagers had some crab legs to put into the pot. The traveler stirred and stirred and stirred. Then he sniffed the stew and said,

> Stir and slosh, through and through
> This is how we make shoe stew

He stirred and stirred and sniffed the stew. Then the traveler said, "I don't want to clam up, but some clams would make this shoe stew the finest in all the seven seas!"

And wonder of wonders, one of the villagers had some clams to put into the pot. The traveler stirred and stirred and stirred. Then he sniffed the stew and said,

> Stir and slosh, through and through
> This is how we make shoe stew

He stirred and stirred and sniffed the stew. Then the traveler said, "I have a rough idea. Some roughy would make this shoe stew the finest in all the seven seas!"

And wonder of wonders, one of the villagers had some roughy to put into the pot. The traveler stirred and stirred and stirred. Then he sniffed the stew and said,

> Stir and slosh, through and through
> This is how we make shoe stew

He stirred and stirred and sniffed the stew. Then the traveler said, "I don't want you to run short, but a little shrimp would make this shoe stew the finest in all the seven seas!"

And wonder of wonders, one of the villagers had some shrimp to put into the pot.

Now the shoe stew began to smell wonderful. The people of the village gathered around the pot. Then they ran home and brought bowls and napkins and bread and cider. They set a long table by the pot and waited for the shoe stew.

When the traveler said the shoe stew was ready, everyone had some. It was delicious, the finest in all the seven seas! And everyone had enough to eat.

As the traveler started to leave the villagers said, "You can't go. We need your shoe to make shoe stew."

The traveler smiled. "Don't worry. Any shoe will do." And he left town.

Late that afternoon, the traveler came to the next little seaside village with nothing but the shirt on his back and the shoes on his feet. He longed to take the weight off his feet and have something to eat. But the people in the town told him the fishing had been very bad that day and there was nothing in the town to eat at all.

Instead of complaining the traveler said, "Let me help you, then. I'll show you how to make a stew so you will never be hungry again. We'll make stew from my (pause) shirt!"

Literature Enrichment Activities
Writing Activity

Noodle Soup Starter

Using the lasagne noodle pattern on page 102, cut enough noodles out of paper for each child. Copy these story starters onto the noodle shapes. Children complete each story.

Story starter 1: Clarissa was cleaning the silverware one day when she found a magic spoon. It could grant her anything she wished.

Story starter 2: Jim told his family he had a magic recipe that would make soup out of a _____.

Story starter 3: The village would never be hungry again once the pot started to cook _____.

Speaking Activities

Oodles of Noodles
(chant)

Many of the cooking-pot stories deal with cooking pots that overflow with rice or pasta. Invite children to join you in this activity game about a pot of noodles that just won't stop. The leader speaks a line, the children repeat it, and do the action indicated.

Let's cook some noodles
Put one in the pot.
Stir and stir and stir and stir.
How many have we got?
2, 4, 6, 8
 (Point to a few children to roll hands one over the other.)

Stir and stir and stir and stir.
How many have we got?
20, 40, 60, 80
 (Add a few more children rolling hands.)

Stir and stir and stir and stir.
How many have we got?
2000, 4000, 6000, 8000
 (Add a few more children rolling hands.)

(Oodles of Noodles chant continues on page 103.)

Oodles of Noodles—*Continued*

> Stir and stir and stir and stir.
> How many have we got?
> 2 million, 4 million, 6 million, 8 million
> > (All children rolling hands.)
>
> Noodles on the ceiling
> Noodles on the floor
> Noodles on the window sill
> Bubbling out the door
>
> What to do with noodles
> Boiling from the pot?
> Eat and eat and eat and eat.
> How many have we got?
> Kids eating noodles
> Boiling from the pot.
> > (Point to children to pretend to eat.)

Just a Soup Song
(Tune: "My Bonnie Lies Over the Ocean")

> My soup pot is starting to simmer
> It's bubbling over the top
> Look out it is running all over
> I can't find the words to say STOP
>
> Whoa back. Halt. Cease.
> Stop what you're doing right now I say.
> E-nough. End this.
> You can't go on bubbling this way.

Related Craft

Hodge Podge Collage

Using the pattern on page 104, cut out a black soup pot for each child. Children mount the pot on white paper and make a collage. First, they put in a picture of their own magic object (shoe, nail, stone) as the "soup starter." Then they can add items such as pieces of corn, rice, macaroni, beans. Or let the soup become fanciful by adding feathers, buttons, shells or leaves. What is the soup of the day?

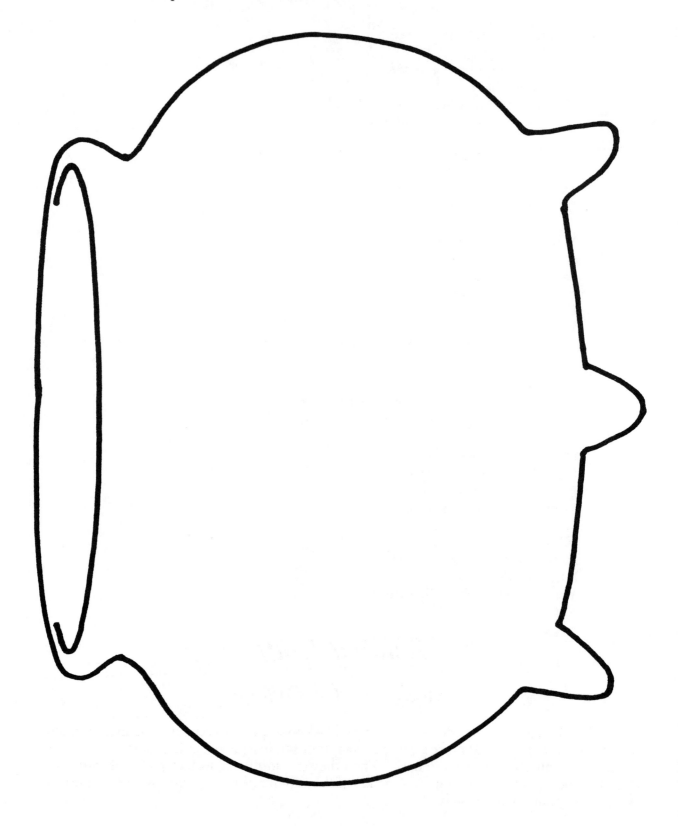

Related Games

Hot Pot

Try to locate an old-fashioned cooking pot to show the children. Remember the sequence of food added to the pot in the stone soup story. Play this game like the traditional hot potato game, passing the potato around a circle of children as if the potato were too hot to handle. Have the children sit in a large circle. Give three children potatoes to pass as music is played. When the music stops, the children holding the potatoes move to the center of the circle as they "put the potatoes in the pot." For the next rounds, pass three carrots, three onions, and three stalks of celery. The pot should be very full by now, so lead the children to tables to enjoy bowls of soup.

Mystery Soup

Cut pictures of food from magazines in preparation for this game. Have children form a circle. One child stands in the center as the leader tapes a picture of food on his or her back. The child in the center may ask questions of the other children about the food. The questions must ask for facts only. (For example: Is my food green?) Older children will find the game more challenging if they ask only questions that can be answered by yes or no. When the person in the center guesses the food, he or she chooses a new person for the center and play continues.

Related Skit

Noodle Pot

Characters:

> funny old woman
> helper
> townspeople
> noodles

Plot: The woman has a magic pot to make noodles. She practices the magic words to make the pot start ("Oodles of noodles fill my pot.") and stop ("Oodles of noodles you can stop.").

The helper hears the words to start the pot, but not to stop it. While the funny old woman is napping, the helper tries out the pot. The noodles bubble over the pot and onto the floor, out the door, into town, and all over everything. When the funny woman wakes up there is a big mess. The helper has to clean up the mess.

Note: In this skit, the children know the basic storyline and they create their own lines of dialogue as they think the characters might say them.

Simple props and costumes will add interest to the presentation. Children playing the noodles start out in the pot, climb over the side, and roll around on the floor. They can wear white T-shirts and tights. Make "noodle" costumes by cutting white garbage bags into strips starting at the open end, and stopping short of the closed end to make a long fringe. Cut a neck hole in the closed end.

Make a large cut-out cardboard pot with a tab fastened to the back so it will stand.

Related Stone Soup Activities
(from other Irving and Currie books)

1. "Out of This World Soup," in *Mudluscious* (Libraries Unlimited, 1986), 117-122.

2. "Magic Microwave," in *Mudluscious* (Libraries Unlimited, 1986), 150-153.

Author and Title Index

About the Authors

JAN IRVING

Jan Irving has been a teacher, a children's librarian, and a visiting professor of children's library services at the University of Iowa's School of Library Science. She was a 1984 recipient of the Putnam Publishing Award, sponsored by the Association for Library Service to Children of the American Library Association. In addition to the five books (*Mudluscious*, *Glad Rags*, *Full Speed Ahead*, *Raising the Roof*, and *From the Heart*) with Robin Currie, Jan has authored *Fanfares: Programs for Classrooms and Libraries* for Libraries Unlimited, and coordinated the state summer library programs for the State Library of Iowa. She is currently a consultant for Children's Library Services, State Library of Iowa. Jan lives in Des Moines.

ROBIN CURRIE

Robin Currie has been active in state-wide children's library services, coordinating the development of summer programs in Iowa and Illinois. She has been a regional consultant for the Illinois State Library and head of Youth Services at Palatine Public Library. In addition to the five books (*Mudluscious*, *Glad Rags*, *Full Speed Ahead*, *Raising the Roof*, and *From the Heart*) with Jan Irving, Robin has written two books for the Iowa State Library: *Rainbows and Ice Cream: Storytimes About Things Kids Like*, and *Double Rainbows: More Storytimes About Things Kids Like*. Robin lives in the Chicago suburbs and manages the children's book department at Anderson's Bookshop in Elmhurst. She is currently a graduate student at the Lutheran School of Theology at Chicago studying for the ordained ministry.